T0360846

The Economics of Intellectual Property and Openness

This book focuses on the economic aspects of intellectual property (IP). It includes considerations of the wider category of intangible assets. However, the primary focus is devoted to patents which the author argues are the most vivid example of the Tragedy of Intangible Abundance (TIA).

TIA touches upon a key issue in the contemporary economy. On the one hand, there is an enormous supply of IP, yet, on the other hand, such an abundance does not necessarily solve existing issues but rather creates new ones as well. This book elaborates on the reasons for the emergence of TIA and its consequences. The author uses clear metaphors to explain very complex issues. The book provides a valuable and interdisciplinary analysis of the field and offers practical solutions. It is based on the data collected by the author during the qualitative research he conducted among a group of start-ups. It presents guidance on determining which instrument is the most efficient for a particular situation. It also provides arguments for decision-makers and their advisors as to why a more open approach towards intellectual property would be more beneficial under many circumstances in the contemporary economy. While universal issues are addressed, the author distinguishes the European perspective too.

The book is written in a clear and concise style and covers all of the crucial aspects of IP management. It will find an audience among scholars of economics and business.

Bartłomiej Biga is an Assistant Professor in the Public Economy and Administration Faculty of Cracow University of Economics, Poland.

Routledge Focus on Economics and Finance

The fields of economics are constantly expanding and evolving. This growth presents challenges for readers trying to keep up with the latest important insights. Routledge Focus on Economics and Finance presents short books on the latest big topics, linking in with the most cutting-edge economics research.

Individually, each title in the series provides coverage of a key academic topic, whilst collectively the series forms a comprehensive collection across the whole spectrum of economics.

The Political Economy of Financial Development in Malaysia
From the Asian Crisis to 1MDB
Lena Rethel

Foreign Exchange Rates
A Research Overview of the Latest Prediction Techniques
Arif Orçun Söylemez

Islamic Economics and COVID-19
The Economic, Social and Scientific Consequences of a Global Pandemic
Masudul Alam Choudhury

The Economics of Intellectual Property and Openness
The Tragedy of Intangible Abundance
Bartłomiej Biga

For more information about this series, please visit www.routledge.com/Routledge-Focus-on-Economics-and-Finance/book-series/RFEF

The Economics
of Intellectual Property
and Openness
The Tragedy of Intangible Abundance

Bartłomiej Biga

Routledge
Taylor & Francis Group

LONDON AND NEW YORK

First published 2021
by Routledge
2 Park Square, Milton Park, Abingdon, Oxon OX14 4RN

and by Routledge
605 Third Avenue, New York, NY 10017

Routledge is an imprint of the Taylor & Francis Group, an informa business

British Library Cataloguing-in-Publication Data
A catalogue record for this book is available from the British Library

Library of Congress Cataloging-in-Publication Data
Names: Biga, Bartłomiej, author.
Title: The economics of intellectual property and openness :
the tragedy of intangible abundance / Bartłomiej Biga.
Description: Milton Park, Abingdon, Oxon ; New York, NY :
Routledge, 2021. |
Series: Routledge focus on economics and finance |
Includes bibliographical references and index.
Subjects: LCSH: Intellectual property. | Intellectual
property—Economic aspects.
Classification: LCC K1401 .B54 2021 (print) |
LCC K1401 (ebook) | DDC 346.04/8—dc23
LC record available at https://lccn.loc.gov/2020051020
LC ebook record available at https://lccn.loc.gov/2020051021

ISBN 13: 978-0-367-56565-7 (hbk)
ISBN 13: 978-0-367-56566-4 (pbk)

Typeset in Times New Roman
by codeMantra

Contents

About the author

In my capacity as a professional I convince people that economics is beautiful, law does not have to be boring, and a scientist may speak comprehensibly. I lecture at universities, cooperate with businesses, maintain a blog and a podcast, and work at the Analysis Centre of the Jagiellonian Club (a non-political association seeking to improve the world of politics). I primarily deal with intellectual property and other intangible assets, behavioural economics, and the economic analysis of law and digital economy.

I know that a couple of those issues sound either formidable or horribly boring. But let's give them a chance – they are not like that immanently by themselves! Too many people simply try to treat economics and law as the secret knowledge that is accessible to a limited number of people who miraculously managed not to fall asleep during (some) boring lectures or while reading (some) boring books.

Economics and law are beautiful, indeed, and may be useful. All of my professional engagements aim at proving that. I deliver knowledge from university to companies, politicians, and all those who enjoy learning what economics is all about. That does not obviously mean that all in economics is simple. Moreover, there are many mechanisms that (hardly) anyone understands, although it is fairly impossible to find an economist who would openly admit that.

I co-create the economic movement Open Eyes Economy that may be summarised as the movement away from the common style of thinking in business 'any income is good, any cost is bad'. My work is based not only on economics and law. I also try – as much as I can – to draw abundantly from psychology, sociology, or neurobiology. I advise strategies of intangible resource management that take advantage of business models based on widespread conditional disclosure.

I believe that knowledge popularisation requires an approachable form, hence the blogging, podcasting, or delivering lectures for varied listeners.

I am professionally engaged in five major fields in my capacity as a:

- university staff member (the Cracow University of Economics, the AGH University of Science and Technology, the SWPS University)
- co-creator of the economic equity movement Open Eyes Economy (oees.pl)
- think tank expert (the Analysis Centre of the Jagiellonian Club)
- mass media commentator for a range of radio and TV broadcasters, public and private)
- the author of the Practical Economics Blog (bartlomiejbiga.pl/blog) and the Non-obvious Knowledge Podcast (bartlomiejbiga.pl/wiedza)

My work focuses on the economic analysis of law and public policies – in theoretical terms (research), in practicable terms (implementation), and in terms of publicity (media).

I pay most of my attention to intellectual property – mainly copyright and patents. Majority of my research is conducted based on the economic analysis of law. It aims at searching for greatest effectiveness of legal regulations (the highest possible benefit-cost ratio).

My majors and areas of scientific interest:

- economic analysis of law
- intellectual property law (protection of inventions and copyright law)
- effectiveness of public policies
- behavioural economics
- corporate intangible resources management
- digital economy

Acknowledgements

The publication is co-financed by the Ministry of Science and Higher Education of Poland within "Regional Initiative of Excellence" Programme for 2019 -2022. Project no.: 021/RID/2018/19. Total financing: 11 897 131,40 PLN.

Introduction

This book explains why the current enormous supply of intellectual property does not only utterly fail to address a number of outstanding issues but also creates new ones. Hence the subtitle 'Tragedy of Intangible Abundance', despite the fact that such a statement may surprise many economists, for whom 'economics is the science of attempting to make optimum use of scarce resources to satisfy needs which, by contrast, are numerous and unlimited'. Therefore, economists find it so difficult to put the words 'tragedy' and 'abundance' in one sentence, because scarcity has been a challenge they strove to solve for years. In consequence, if 'abundance' appears, according to many of them, such a state must be the opposite of 'tragedy'.

Unfortunately, the analysis of the contemporary economy indicates that, in the case of intellectual property, abundance may cause a range of problems. In order to partially mitigate the adverse impact of that phenomenon, openness-derived constructs should be disseminated – i.e. those that provide for relatively widespread but contingent accessibility to intellectual property instead of relying mainly on exclusive rights (patents, copyright with 'All Rights Reserved', etc.). That approach is referred herein to as 'Directed Diffusion'. It defines a number of tools that permit the development of effective business models based on more open intellectual property management. Hence the book has been titled: 'The Economics of Intellectual Property and Openness'.

The benefits arising from a more open approach to intellectual property are indicated by a number of authors (Murray: 2016vx, Parker: 2018tt, Christen: 2012vl, Henkel: 2014tb, Peters: 2010wl, Drechsler: 2012tq, Chesbrought: 2004ds, Pollock: 2018uf, Foray: 2013vp). However, the aim of this book is also to comprehensively explain the circumstances that justify greater openness as well as to identify specific constructs that may be used for the purpose of business models of companies operating in various industries.

It is also worth mentioning that in the history of economic sciences, on several occasions the term 'tragedy' has been used for describing only certain fragments of reality. It is not so much about specific dramatic events but about the state of relations between respective actors, which is a kind of a trap due to a specific combination of stimuli: it leads to suboptimal outcomes but the existing incentive systems are useless to overcome them. Thus, respective actors, striving to maximise their own utility, contribute to the development of constructs that are not beneficial to the general public and in a sense to themselves too. It is about a typical tension within the framework of non-cooperative games – although abandoning some actions would be beneficial to the general public, everyone opts for a non-cooperative option because no one knows how others will behave and the system puts a non-cooperating entity in a relatively better situation (classic prisoner's dilemma).

That is somewhat surprising, however, because game theory sees the possibility of changing the prisoner's dilemma into a cooperative game when everyone knows ahead of time that the game will be repeated an indefinite number of times. Then – as a model would indicate – respective prisoners should initially apply a cooperative strategy, and then tit for tat. Yet, observations indicate that this mechanism is unable to break the tragedy described in this book. This is probably due to excessive complexity within the system – the number of actors and the perception of public (or quasi-public) goods.

The research perspective of this book falls within the economic analysis of law (Law and Economics). It implies that law is equivalent to any other subject matter of economic study, and therefore the book focuses on the effectiveness of legal regulations, and specifically the ones governing intellectual property. However, a number of issues extend beyond purely legislative aspects, and that is why this study also elaborates upon actual activities or business models that reach beyond law and related regulations.

The structure of the book starts with the Tragedy of Intangible Abundance being placed among other tragedies described in economic sciences. The causes of its emergence and the most important manifestations of its occurrence are analysed. On this basis, it is possible to analyse ways to counteract the 'Tragedy of Intangible Abundance'. Although systemic solutions are discussed in the book, the emphasis is put on bottom-up activities that are feasible at the level of individual enterprises. This is due to the belief that far-reaching changes in international intellectual property regimes are very unlikely due to complex conflicts of interest. However, changes are possible in enterprise business models.

This book is the outcome of the study conducted within the framework of the Open Eyes Economy – an international movement devoted to economy based on social values (www.oees.pl/en), founded in 2015 in Kraków, Poland. The book falls within one of the research pathways within the framework of this movement – 'Commons and Commoning', undertaken by an international expert group established in 2019 in Vienna. The book utilises secondary, bibliographical research and own, primary research projects within the OEES movement.

In summary, the main goal of this study is to analyse the adverse impact of an overly closed approach to intellectual property management and to indicate the profitability of a more open approach based on business models that take advantage of common but contingent accessibility to intellectual property. The subtitle 'Tragedy of Intangible Abundance' is a trap. But it is not a trap without a way out.

1   Tragedies in economics

1.1 Economics of scarcity

Economics is said to be the science of managing the attempt to make optimum use of scarce resources to satisfy numerous and unlimited needs. Within this context, the association 'scarce good equals a high value good' seems to be fully legitimate. This approach may even be useful when trying to explain the Aristotelian water and diamond paradox. The latter, being much scarcer, is much more valuable although, unlike water, it is not necessary for life. Economists are accustomed to the strong correlation between scarcity and price. However, problems arose with the growing importance of intellectual property, in the case of which any scarcity is obviously out of the question. Furthermore, thanks to the networking effect, the abundance (as an antonym of scarcity) of any construct is positively correlated with value. There are also no physical restrictions on how many people can take advantage of one construct at the same time. Therefore, without strong regulatory interference, the natural state here is the lack of competitiveness in consumption and the inability to exclude from consumption. Thus, we are here dealing with something that fits the definition of public goods.

This circumstance raises concerns among many entrepreneurs and creators. In their simplified reasoning, this prevents effective monetisation of the invention, design or artistic work, often referred to as 'intellectual goods'. Since – in the traditional sense – value is positively correlated with scarcity, attempts are made to artificially create this scarcity using legal monopolies. Such a decision is usually not preceded by an analysis of alternative methods of managing intellectual property, which – as the subject of this study – are in many cases much more effective. Especially in the digital economy, attempts to counteract the ease of copying intellectual property are doomed to failure, being associated with the need to incur significant costs, and yet will still lead to unsatisfactory results.

This phenomenon is the root cause of the Tragedy of Intangible Abundance. A number of other factors are obviously necessary for it to occur, which are discussed in the next section. However, without mindlessly reaching (or even abusing) legal monopolies in the management of intellectual property, the problem addressed in this book would not have reached such a large scale (Lemley, 2019).

Economists are not the only ones who have found it difficult to find their place in the world dominated by intangible assets. In addition, Accountants have not yet developed satisfactory methods of valuing what cannot be touched or – often – even sold. The problem with intangible resources is that although they play a key role in enterprises, they are not fully controlled (owned) by them, which is particularly evident in the example of human capital. In addition, a large part of reporting is not subordinated to the desire to learn about the actual state of the company, but tax optimisation (Černíková, 2018).

The third professional group, which plays an important role in the context of intellectual property – lawyers – also contributes to the Tragedy of Intangible Abundance. Transferring too much power to legal departments – especially in the face of shortcomings in the strategic management of intellectual property – almost always means excessive patenting and protection of works in the traditional formula of 'All Rights Reserved'. The area of legal monopolies is a natural environment for representatives of this profession, while abandonment of such tools carries the risk of reducing the demand for legal services. Moreover, in organisations unaware of modern methods of managing intellectual property, it is much easier to attribute responsibility (guilt) for failure in a situation where some intellectual property was not subjected to any protection, rather than when a patent has been granted but did not assure satisfactory settlement in court.

As a result, as J. Low and P. C. Kalafut (2006, p. 37) wrote, investors must flounder in the dark. The aforementioned habits and brachylogy have led to the construction of such a system of stimuli in organisations that the most rational behaviour of its individual units is to stick to the existing paths of intellectual property management in the form of legal monopolies. Therefore, scarcity is created in an artificial way, which goes against the nature of intellectual property. Thousands of such individual decisions summarily construct the Tragedy of Intangible Abundance.

When moving the analysis to a higher level, of respective sectors of the economy, it is plausible to state that the game resembles the situation of evolutionary enlargement of the peacock's tail described by R. Frank (2012). It is to bring a relative advantage over competitors but the monstrous size of the tails (patents) make the entire species (sector) more and more dysfunctional. As a result, even if there is a perception of attractiveness of alternative methods of intellectual property management in a company, due to the competitors' comprehensive patent portfolios, it is not easy to make a decision about taking a different path. This is because it may entail exposure to lawsuits, since competitors are encouraged to do so due to low risk of a possible counterclaim, and will therefore effectively deter, due to the unpredictability of court decisions. Thus, companies are trapped: they patent not to maximise benefits but to minimise losses.

We now face a situation where, as a result of increasing the role of intellectual property in the economy, the possibility of addressing the basic tragedy of scarcity in economy has appeared, but key professional groups have undertaken a number of actions to limit the availability of intangible goods in order to maintain the state of scarcity, the basis for century-old business models. Therefore, those two tragedies – scarcity and abundance – although seemingly contradictory, cannot be considered separately. The above-mentioned activities cause scarcity to be promoted in key areas, while abundance (or even excess) appears in the areas of lesser value, which adversely affects the entire situation related to intellectual property management in the contemporary economy.

1.2 Tragedy of the Commons

The problem of the possible depletion of public goods was noticed in the economy in 1832 thanks to W. F. Lloyd. However, it entered public consciousness only after having been described by the biologist G. Hardin (1968). He pointed out that if there were too many cows grazing on common meadows, then the pasture could be destroyed – there was not enough time to let it grow back.

For a lot of people, this was a shocking observation. Common pastures were seen as public goods, which – without prejudice to others – may be used by all stakeholders. However, it is in the common interest of the entire community not to feed more cows than the restoration capacity of the meadow allows. The interests of individual farmers, on the other hand, lead them to increase the number of cows, as this allows them to increase their individual benefits. Thinking about the common good in this case is more difficult because without effective coordination mechanisms, a farmer who will stick to his limit has no guarantee that other users will not continue to sterilise the pasture in pursuit of their personal interests.

This, in turn, encourages not to define such pastures as 'public goods' (which in the broad sense of the category is not a mistake) but call them 'commons'. It is admittedly not possible to ban their usage but there is certain competitiveness at stake because – as the example described by Hardin indicates – those goods may be depleted, which is out of question in the case of goods which are completely public (such as information). And such a statement should, in principle, end the discussion on the possibility of extrapolating the insights described in the Tragedy of the Commons onto intellectual property, which cannot be exhausted or worn out.

For this reason a free-rider problem that may arise in relation to intellectual property is not the same as in the case of joint pasture. Here, a person who intensively uses a given resource – 'more than he or she deserves' – does not directly restrict the benefits of others who adhere to the rules on the intensity of use. There will not be less information for others. The intensity of usage is not a problem here.

This does not mean, however, that a free rider will not gain indirectly a certain advantage. It might be exemplified by competition among photographers – the one who does not bear the cost of purchasing expensive, specialised image processing software and uses them without a licence can offer a better price for his or her services. This effect, however, will be rather small – licence fees represent only a small part of the costs, and the work on unauthorised software copies is increasingly less effective (lack of access to technical support or the producer's cloud-based solutions). In the case of intellectual property, being a free rider can therefore give a certain individual advantage, which must also mean some harm to those entities that follow the rules.

Some authors (Lemley, 2004, p. 1033), however, indicate that no advantage is achieved, and in this case the rhetoric of a free-rider problem is a mistake. As a model, it focuses on counteracting negative externalities, the costs suffered by a third party. This is because in the case of material ownership, one often has a zero-sum game – 'if I use a piece of land, you can't use it. If I overgraze the commons, that overgrazing imposes costs on anyone else who might use the commons' (Lemley, 2004, p. 1033). Therefore, the purpose of property rights is to counteract such negative externalities by internalising them.

On the other hand, in the case of intellectual property we should rather talk about positive externalities. Therefore there is no need for institutional activities to internalise them. The basic externality in relation to intellectual property has a network character: the more valuable the construct is for a given user, the more people use the same. In the example of photographic services cited above, using the same software (e.g. CorelDRAW or Photoshop) will mean lower transaction costs when establishing cooperation among photographers. For the manufacturer of such software, the fact of being a creator of a standard in a given industry is a huge competitive advantage, e.g. Microsoft Word, which, although commonly copied without authorisation, determines the market power of the manufacturer due to the overall number of its legal and illegal users.

M. Boldrin and D. Levine (Boldrin & Levine, 2008, p. 167) point out that only fully abstract things are beyond any competition and may be fully recognised as public goods. Implementations and specific applications are not entitled to be called by that name. They illustrate this with an example of coffee – the fact that I drink it does not essentially limit your ability to drink coffee – and here there is no need for legal intervention. However, if someone would like to drink my coffee from my cup, it will be just a theft.

Initially, it has been pointed out that the only implications of G. Hardin's concept may be either the privatisation of public goods or the extension of full guardianship by the Leviathan State (Gross & De Dreu, 2019). It is noted that this has been the most suggestive economic metaphor since A. Smith's 'invisible hand'. They were read together because they were claimed to encompass two fundamental categories of situations – when individual choices lead to effective decisions (Smith) and when they lead to the opposite situation (Hardin). The works by E. Ostrom (Ostrom, 2015) provided the breakthrough as they showed that in such situations effective solutions may also appear as a result of bottom-up activities by the interested communities.

Today, however, Wikipedia is the most striking example of a collective institution for shared resource management. This is the story of the incredible success of grassroots knowledge generation and sharing. It is worth emphasising that its success was achieved not despite – but thanks to – the application of the principle of openness of resources (the content is made available under free Creative Commons licences). The possibility of copying them easily and legally is not a discouragement for authors to contribute, but for many it actually offers a fundamental incentive.

According to Ostrom, the existence of such situations requires the fulfilment of certain institutional conditions. First, it indicates the clarity of law (who is empowered to do what, who can impose what penalties). Furthermore, this law must be widely accepted by the community, which requires the creation of tools for joint, democratic decision-making by all those using the given resources. Second, conflict resolution mechanisms must be both local and public. The inclusion and participation of community members is necessary because they have the greatest interest in making management effective and know best how to circumvent common principles. Thirdly, the rules must not conflict with higher-order regulations. So, solutions break out from the two-dimensional tension between state and private property.

In terms of the differences outlined above, it is difficult to demonstrate the legitimacy of a wider extrapolation of insights related to the Tragedy of the Commons to intellectual property. It is not without reason that Hardin and Ostrom give hardly any space to it at all. As it has already been mentioned, the main difference is due to the nature of the externalities that occur, which are in principle only positive in relation to intellectual property. This also makes the free-rider problem much less severe for society.

What is, however, useful in the context of the Theory of Intangible Abundance, according to Ostrom, is the opportunity to ensure partial, bottom-up breaking through ineffective Nash equilibriums in non-cooperative games. Such activities in the field of intellectual property also appear – patent pools, cross licensing, standardisation organisations, etc. Their role, however, is underappreciated, and the opportunity to participate is usually limited to the largest players in a given market. Those actions may therefore only reduce the scale of both tragedies discussed in this book, but they certainly cannot be treated as a comprehensive solution.

1.3 Tragedy of the Anti-Commons

The Tragedy of the Anti-Commons is the subsequent blatantly obvious issue to be analysed. That concept was presented by M. Heller (1998). He described it by means of the example of Moscow apartments, which were privatised after the collapse of the Soviet Union. However, as a general rule, several families lived in large apartments. Each family was granted ownership of a separate room and joint ownership of the common areas – kitchen, corridor, etc. Such real estate (often in a very convenient location) would be extremely valuable as a whole. In other words, the achievable price for a one-off sale of the entire apartment would be much higher than the sum of ownership rights resold by the families who shared them.

That phenomenon described by M. Heller defines the situation in which each of the owners has the right to exclude the others from using the resource but no one has the entitlement to use it in its entirety.

And that very aptly describes the situation that is brought about by the aberration of intellectual property law in innovation-based sectors. Patents particularly give the right to exclude others from using a particular solution. However, due to the intensity of patenting in some sectors, a huge number of those rights give rise to a patent thicket. It means that larger projects such as operating systems, advanced electronic devices, etc., may potentially infringe so many patents that their creator, even if possessing a notable portfolio of intellectual property, often fails to effectively utilise own resources.

For years, the practice of operating Patent Offices, which grant exclusive rights to banal ideas and solutions, has led to the situation similar to the one in privatised apartments caused by the Russian authorities. One can – relatively effectively – exclude others from using but nobody can fully (and thus effectively) utilise the resources. From the point of view of the objectives of this book, noticing this mechanism is extremely important, although it is insufficient to fully explain the subject matter. The problem of fragmentation of property is only one of the elements that have led to the Tragedy of Intangible Abundance. It also shows the conceptual weakness in treating property mainly in negative categories – i.e. opportunities for exclusion.

This example shows that ownership may appropriately fulfil its function if it sufficiently assures the entitlement to exercise positive rights particularly in terms of usage and also of derivable benefits. However, it is also necessary to add a context of obligation related to ownership, which, after all, cannot be treated as an unlimited right. Obligation – a category broader than the legal concept of liability – is a natural consequence of the privileges associated with ownership rights. Moreover, those obligations are not mere duties on the part of the liable, but they allow for coordination of activities that may be beneficial for each owner.

That mechanism applies to both traditional property – land development regulations protecting neighbours – and intellectual property, in particular, in the context of standardisation measures. It was the lack of such coordination that led to the tragedy described by M. Heller. For this reason, his analysis is addressed primarily to the state because market mechanisms are insufficient (Heller, 1998, p. 688). Even if rights are well-defined, transaction costs, downtime, rent-seeking will still bring huge losses. Over time, the market may create formal and informal institutions that will allow to achieve effective 'bundles of rights'. Heller (1998, p. 688) notes, however, that in a situation where the Tragedy of the Anti-Commons is allowed to occur in some area, the actions of the government may also be doomed to failure. Therefore, his recommendations focus on preventing the separation of positive and negative ownership right bundles.

Those problems, when related to intellectual property, seem to be even more significant, because the basic goal of the legal regulations is to strive for the widest possible dissemination – the diffusion of innovation. The temporary monopoly is only a means to encourage creators to act and reveal the effects of their work. Due to the peculiarity of that type of activity, which is manifested primarily in the overbuilding and improvement of previous constructs, and due to the blurry boundaries of respective rights, the legal system, which focuses more on exclusion from usage than on positive ownership rights, must be called dysfunctional. A system whose fundamental function is dissemination must operate in the opposite direction.

1.4 Tragedy of Intangible Abundance

The Tragedy of Intangible Abundance is a description of a crucial problem in the contemporary economy. One may see a contradiction in the combination of the words 'tragedy' and 'abundance'. However, the contradiction is only illusory. Its perception is the result of economists' deeply rooted approach in which the essence of management is to combat scarcity. For many, permanent scarcity is the basic concept in economics, in the context of which economics is understood to make optimum use of scarce resources to satisfy unlimited human needs (as discussed in the Introduction chapter. In that sense, abundance cannot be associated with tragedy because the actual occurrence of abundance would mean the solution for this seemingly immanent tragedy.

The above reasoning worked well in an economy dominated by tangible assets. However, today, in the digital era, abundance (or even excess) is something completely natural. That is due to the possibility of non-competitive use of the same assets, due to the ease with which they can be copied. Access to intellectual resources may be – and often is – restricted mainly based on legal monopolies. However, that is an artificial state that must be created based on specific regulatory frameworks and a series of decisions and actions by entities possessing some intangible resources. Therefore, abundance in this sense does not need to be created and institutionally supported. It is a natural consequence of changes taking place in business.

However, why abundance is seen in terms of tragedy needs to be clarified. There are four main reasons:

1   The supply of intellectual property is not tailored to demand.
2   Intellectual property law has become an area of the arms race.
3   The low quality of granted exclusive rights creates patent thickets and is a breeding ground for trolls.
4   Companies are trapped – in the face of ineffectiveness of intellectual property rights they patent more and more not to maximise benefits but to minimise losses.

1.4.1 The supply of intellectual property is not tailored to demand

A huge amount of intellectual property is being created in the contemporary economy. It cannot be denied that society also shows very high demand for it. The problem is that the demand only slightly coincides with what appears in circulation. That regularity may be observed even by analysing the pharmaceutical industry. The companies operating in this industry concentrate a significant part of their activities on simple painkillers / anti-inflammatory drugs, which do not differ much from one another and remedy mainly trivial, although common, ailments. The major difference between those products made by diverse manufacturers comes down to the trade mark since the composition is almost identical as is the active ingredient.

Investments in promoting a specific pharmaceutical product of a given type are very profitable for those companies. However, this is done at the expense of research on completely new categories of pharmaceuticals the market for which, even if they are to remedy the most serious diseases, is incomparably smaller, and the process of creating and obtaining regulatory approvals may be long and unpredictable. So, we have a huge supply of intellectual property (in this case mainly related to anti-inflammatory drug trademarks) but many serious health problems remain unresolved (demand side).

On the one hand, it is plausible to state that this is a standard demand-supply response. Painkillers/anti-inflammatory drugs are bought much more often, so the appearance of a corresponding supply is obvious. However, money 'dissipating' for those activities does not convert into improvements among the sick. Only new, innovative pharmaceutical products may bring about a major change. They are obviously created but that process is slowed down because a significant part of the resources of the pharmaceutical sector is directed elsewhere (for trademark marketing).

That observation is confirmed by the analysis of more cross-sectoral data. As the estimates arising from the Intangible Asset Market Value Study (Graph 1.1) show, a very dynamic increase in the percentage share of intangible resources in the value of the largest American companies has been observed in consecutive decades.

It is worth comparing this data with the estimates of the World Intellectual Property Organization (WIPO) regarding the value added of products sold worldwide (Graph 1.2). This study admittedly covers a much shorter period and is not limited to the 500 largest American companies, and therefore the possibilities for comparing data are very limited. However, it is possible to observe that, unlike the percentage share of intangible resources in the value of companies, the percentage share of intangible resources in the value of goods sold does not increase but remains stable. That statement is true regardless of how we treat the WIPO category 'work' – i.e. whether we include it in tangible or intangible resources – because this component also remains at a similar level.

That justifies the conclusion that although intangible resources appear to an increasing extent and constitute an increasingly important component of companies (Ocean Tomo's study), it does not translate into an increased share in creating the value of goods sold (WIPO study). Thus, there is an increasing supply of them, but it does not respond to reported demand. That leads to the conclusion that

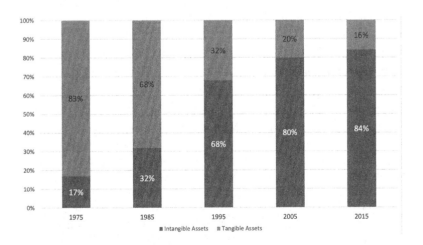

Graph 1.1 Components of S&P 500 market value.
Source: Ocean Tomo (2015).

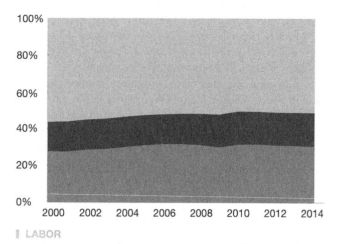

Graph 1.2 Value added as a percentage of the total value of all products manufactured and sold worldwide.
Source: World Intellectual Property Organization (WIPO) (2017).

enterprises have a problem with commercialising intellectual property or that a large part of generated/reported intellectual property is intended to be used for speculating on the company's valuation.

1.4.2 Intellectual property law has become an area of the arms race

The analysis of the strategies of the largest companies that base their operations on intangible resources indicates that intellectual property law is less and less used for the purposes for which it was created, since in a typical situation legal protection of intellectual property was to encourage the creation and disclosure of the discoveries. Its purpose was to protect smaller and weaker creative entities. The awarded monopoly was to allow sales for a time at a price much higher than marginal costs, which was supposed to allow the creator to reward the expenditure on creating the invention/work. For the general public, this was supposed to be a guarantee of ensuring a high supply of intellectual property in exchange for a temporary limitation in accessibility resulting from the legal monopoly that has been granted.

Nowadays, however, the greatest players in the digital world have turned this area into an arms race. Patents in this sense are primarily to act as a deterrent. Therefore, companies accumulate those exclusive rights not only to exercise such exclusive rights to sell innovative products but also to discourage other players from bringing the case to court against them (Drahos, 2017). This is done by increasing the arsenal of patents that may be utilised in a counterclaim lawsuit. This was the main intention of Google's takeover of Motorola – the most important asset was a comprehensive patent portfolio that allowed Google to protect Android against possible allegations of infringement of the exclusive rights of iOS created by Apple.

Therefore, just like in the Cold War, a significant part of the arsenal is intended only to deter the opponent, and ultimately for the purpose of a strategic counter-offensive. As the study (Lemley & Shapiro, 2005, pp. 75–98) shows, only a few per cent of patents are used commercially. Actual conflicts, when taking into account the volume of patents granted (over a million per year), are relatively rare. Only 1.5% of patents are subject to litigation, and only 0.1% reaches the final judicial stage.

Another aspect by which the arms race metaphor may be adequate is the fact that 46% of disputes end with patent annulment. So this means that much of the 'arsenal' turns out to be dummy munitions. However, when it comes to a dispute and the weapon (patent) turns out to be real and effective, then the range of destruction is very large (even nuclear). The study conducted by PWC (Barry, Arad, Ansell, Cartier, & Lee, 2016) shows that average damages awarded in the cases of intellectual property in the US amount to several million dollars (Graph 1.3).

1.4.3 The low quality of granted exclusive rights creates patent thickets and is a breeding ground for trolls

The Tragedy of Intangible Abundance is even greater because today's system does not solve existing problems (inadequacy of supply to demand) but, in many cases, deepens or even creates new ones. The abundance of patents means the creation of patent thickets, which in a number of industries strongly impede or even, according to some (Gurgula, 2017; Yuan & Li, 2020), prevent one from entering the market. And this is not about creating an exit barrier model ensuring a temporary monopoly to commercialise a particular construct, which is the essence of the domain of law at issue. Intellectual property law in this case, instead of stimulating innovation, curbs its development,

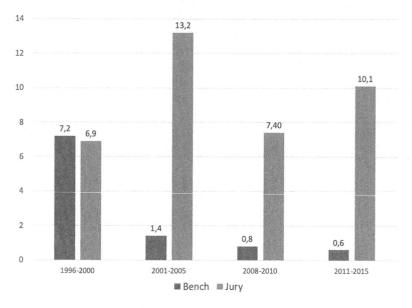

Graph 1.3 Median damages award (in $M): bench vs jury decisions.
Source: Barry et al. (2016, p. 5).

allowing for oligopolisation of significant areas – much broader than it would appear from the sum of the scopes of protection under respective exclusive rights.

The problem is not only the number of patents granted but also their excessively low quality. Unrestricted observance of the requirement of non-obviousness for patentability as well as approval of imprecise patent claims (mainly based on functional claims) means that the limitations on respective exclusive rights are blurred. Therefore, it is one thing to enter the strongly patented market in which one can still pave one's way bypassing the patent-protected areas relatively successfully, rather than – which is the case now – break through the thicket that not only leaves little safe space but also the scopes of respective patents overlap.

Those circumstances ensure that attempts to set up specific business operations are exposed to enormous risk. However, this state of affairs feeds the patent trolls (by some authors Non-Practising Entities – NPE – to avoid the negative connotation of the term 'troll'). Those entities are specialised blackmailers. They come into possession of low quality patents – often cheap, non-specific, which do not have large commercial potential, but the aforementioned imprecision allows one to effectively block large projects of other players.

When creating more complex innovative projects – such as smartphones or operating systems – thousands of constructs are taken advantage of. Therefore, a troll equipped with a patent of indistinctly applied boundaries has considerable room for alleging infringement of its intellectual property and demanding millions in damages. Moreover, even when the likelihood of effective enforcement of such demands in court is assessed to be very low, large companies often buckle under this blackmail. For them, even the risk of delaying the launch of a product (until the court settles the case) would entail much greater losses than compensation paid to a troll. Furthermore, in the face of the imminent unpredictability of court decisions regarding intellectual property, one cannot rule out a troll winning, which in extreme cases could even lead to a ban on sales.

RPX (RPX Corporation, 2019) estimates the direct cost of patent trolls for the US economy to equal $ 7.4 billion, out of which 57% account for legal fees and 43% for settlement and compensation. According to those estimates, the percentage share of litigation filed in the US in the field of intellectual property is approx. 70%. Other estimates are much more conservative (19%), which, however, also shows the considerable scale of the problem.

1.4.4 Companies are trapped – in the face of ineffectiveness of intellectual property rights they patent more and more not to maximise benefits but to minimise losses

The Tragedy of Intangible Abundance is a trap. Many companies patent more and more, not to maximise benefits but to minimise losses. Only 5% of patents generate revenue earned from licence fees (Lemley & Shapiro, 2005). It obviously does not mean that the remaining 95% of patents are useless for an enterprise. They may actually be used only within that one enterprise. However, the enterprises that decided to conduct an in-depth audit of their patents find that a relatively small number of them were actually useful.

The tragedy of this trap therefore arises from the need to incur costs in relation to the huge number of patents, out of which only a small part is used for business purposes. As the unpublished pilot studies conducted as part of Open Eyes Economy show, in many cases entrepreneurs do not take into account the possibility of basing their business strategies on a different model of managing intangible resources. The following mental shortcut is common: if you have something that may be patented/registered and you are considering to market products based on intellectual property, you apply for legal protection (patent, design, trademark, etc.).

At this point, it is important to mention the costs of patenting, which are very high. Therefore, in case a patent turns out to be useless and an enterprise renounces from paying the patent maintenance fees after a couple of years, it will only cut the costs of a progressive maintenance fee payable to Patent Offices. Initial costs (including, above all, preparation of the application form, patent purity search) will therefore simply be sunk costs. A more detailed analysis of those aspects is provided in Chapter 3.

In summary, the Tragedy of Intangible Abundance describes a rather bizarre situation. Partial elimination of the economics of scarcity and consequent replacement with the economics of abundance has not only failed to address classic management concerns but in many cases it has deepened them and brought about new ones. The Tragedy of Intangible Abundance also shows that the supply-demand mechanism alone does not lead to a clearly better satisfaction of needs – so as to speak of a level that could be expected in terms of the current abundance of resources.

In addition, in the digital world, legal methods of protecting intellectual property developed centuries ago have proven extremely ineffective. Attachment to them, resulting from the hasty extrapolation of constructs appropriate for tangible assets to intangible resources has caused deepening dysfunctions to be left outstanding. However, it seems that their scale has already become so large that the motivation to take measures to limit the Tragedy of Intangible Abundance is so strong that in the near future more and more intense attempts to break this trap should be expected. The only course of action is shifting towards more open constructs, which is elaborated upon in Chapter 4.

References

Barry, C., Arad, R., Ansell, L., Cartier, M., & Lee, H. (2016). *2016 Patent Litigation Study: Are We at an Inflection Point?* New York: PricewaterhouseCoopers.

Boldrin, M., & Levine, D. K. (2008). *Against intellectual monopoly* (Vol. 8). Cambridge: Cambridge University Press.

Černíková, M. (2018). Tax optimization of intangible assets in the Czech environment. *Ad Alta: Journal of Interdisciplinary Research, 8*(1), 43–46.

Drahos, P. (2017). The injustice of intellectual property. In *Intellectual Property Forum: journal of the Intellectual and Industrial Property Society of Australia and New Zealand* (No. 110, p. 56). Intellectual and Industrial Property Society of Australia and New Zealand Inc.

Frank, R. H. (2012). *The Darwin economy: Liberty, competition, and the common good*. Princeton, NJ: Princeton University Press.

Gross, J., & De Dreu, C. K. (2019). Individual solutions to shared problems create a modern tragedy of the commons. *Science Advances, 5*(4), eaau7296.

Gurgula, O. (2017). Strategic accumulation of patents in the pharmaceutical industry and patent thickets in complex technologies–two different concepts sharing similar features. *IIC-International Review of Intellectual Property and Competition Law, 48*(4), 385–404.

Hardin, G. (1968). The tragedy of the commons. *Science, 162*(3859), 1243–1248. http://doi.org/10.1126/science.162.3859.1243

Heller, M. (1998). The tragedy of anticommons: Property in the transition from Marx to markets. *Harvard Law Review, 111*(3), 621–688.

Lemley, M. (2019). IP in a world without scarcity. In D. Mendis, M. Lemley, & M. Rimmer (Eds.), *3D Printing and Beyond*. Northampton: Edward Elgar Publishing.

Lemley, M. A. (2004). Property, intellectual property, and free riding. *Texas Law Review, 83*, 1031–1087.

Lemley, M. A., & Shapiro, C. (2005). Probabilistic patents. *The Journal of Economic Perspectives, 19*(2), 75–98.

Low, J., & Kalafut, P. C. (2006). *Niematerialna wartość firmy. Ukryte źródła przewagi konkurencyjnej*. Kraków: Wolters Kluwer.

Ocean Tomo. (2015). *Annual Study of Intangible Asset Market Value* (pp. 1–3). Ocean Tomo. https://www.oceantomo.com/intangible-asset-market-value-study/download/

Ostrom, E. (2015). *Governing the Commons*. Cambridge: Cambridge University Press.

RPX Corporation. (2019). *Patent Litigation and Marketplace Report* (pp. 1–25). RPX.

World Intellectual Property Organization (WIPO). (2017). *World Intellectual Property Report 2017 - Intangible Capital in Global Value Chains* (pp. 1–137). https://www.wipo.int/edocs/pubdocs/en/wipo_pub_944_2017.pdf

Yuan, X., & Li, X. (2020). A network analytic method for measuring patent thickets: A case of FCEV technology. *Technological Forecasting and Social Change, 156*, 120038.

2 What caused the Tragedy of Intangible Abundance

2.1 Low quality of patents

The main reason why it is legitimate to use the term 'tragedy' in the event of an abundance of intellectual property, results from the low average quality of respective exclusive rights, in particular patents. This fact was caused by a number of circumstances for which, however, Patent Offices are primarily responsible (non-restrictive observance of the requirement of non-obviousness, approval of functional reservations, and finally software patenting).

Because Patent Offices apply specific laws, responsibility also lies with legislators to some extent. In this case, however, problems arose as a result of misconduct in the context of discretionary decision-making powers – i.e. as a result of the interpretation of vague terms, the freedom to assess evidence, or in some cases also administrative decisions – and not completely misguided legislation.

The entrepreneurs who often take part in patent racing, thus accelerating the breakneck speed without any deeper reflection, have also contributed to the low quality of patents. In this case, this excessive phenomenon could be combated by legislative amendments, although it is difficult to attribute a substantial part of the blame to law and related regulations. However, it is possible to make a far-reaching change in the pattern of stimuli in the system without imperative influence on strategic decisions of enterprises, which will be addressed later in this chapter.

2.1.1 Low level of non-obviousness

The weakness of a patent does not result from legal provisions as they create a very strong temporary monopoly and – at least in theory – guarantee a number of legal measures for the purpose of exercising these rights. Its weakness results primarily from the activities of Patent Offices, more specifically the abuse of discretionary powers. It is all mainly about unified global regulations, which take advantage of the general clause of the 'degree of inventiveness' also referred to as 'the requirement of non-obviousness'. The excessively liberal understanding of that requirement is the reason for granting protection of merely banal constructs, which in the long run leads to the degradation of the entire intellectual property protection system and is one of the main reasons for the Tragedy of Intangible Abundance.

It is difficult to clearly state why Patent Offices treat the requirement of non-obviousness so liberally. The most likely explanation is the low competence of people who verify application forms, who do not have sufficient knowledge (or substantive support) in specific fields of technology. Hence, a properly constructed description of the patent claim, if it sounds sufficiently convincing, then by the right choice of words alone it can determine the success in obtaining a patent.

In order to obtain a patent, it is therefore necessary to prove that the invention protection that is applied for is compliant with the following provision:

> the state of the art shall be held to comprise everything made available to the public by means of a written or oral description, by use, displaying or disclosure in any other way, before the date according to which priority to obtain a patent is determined.

Such regulations exist in the legal acts of majority of countries that are signatories to international patent agreements. Such a regulatory framework intentionally leaves considerable discretionary powers to a competent authority. Its task is therefore to fill the above-mentioned abstract and general standard formula with a specific factual content. That will directly affect the stage of subsumption (legal qualification), in which the competent authority assesses whether the mandatory requirements for issuing a positive decision have been met.

According to the legislator, 'non-obviousness' means for an expert to be not obvious in terms of the current state of technology. Therefore, there is much room for interpretation – both by the patent office and by the courts. An interesting clarification was proposed by one of the Polish courts – the Voivodeship Administrative Court in Warsaw delivered its judgment on 6 June 2006 deciding that:

> the invention is considered to be not obvious when the essence of the technical problem addressed by the invention is implemented

in particular by: technical means totally different from those identified by the background knowledge within the framework of the
state of the art, which makes it feasible to develop a function of
the purpose of the invention other than the background one or
new technical means and such their mutual structural and functional integration which differs from the commonly recognised
background knowledge, whereby such technical means differ
from the background knowledge in terms of objectives set and the
deliverables.

(VI SA / Wa 454/06, LEX No. 210151)

It does not mean, however, that in terms of current practice, patents are only granted for ground-breaking inventions that considerably contribute to technological advancement. On the contrary, the
non-restrictive interpretation of the requirement of non-obviousness
encourages to apply for a patent even in respect to weak inventions,
which as such do not have innovation potential but may be effectively
used for the purpose of creating patent thickets or within the operations of patent trolls.

There are a number of factors that must be taken into account
when interpreting general clauses such as the 'requirement of
non-obviousness'. It is also expected from the authorities conducting the proceedings that this process will be carried out according
to established standards, the most important of which is the principle of the party's active participation in the proceedings as well as an
exhaustive explanation of actions taken and grounds for decisions
made. Within this framework, however, there remains significant
space for implementing a specific innovation policy. Depending on
the related objectives, a variety of decisions will be deemed appropriate provided that they are kept within the limits of discretionary
powers vested in competent authorities. In other words, it is possible
to tighten the requirement of non-obviousness even without any legislative amendments.

Furthermore, it seems that this is the only viable method of counteracting the Tragedy of Intangible Abundance. Making any far-reaching
amendments to the legal regulations would be extremely difficult or
even impossible. Such amendments would, however, have to be carried
out at the level of international agreements. In this case, however, the
conflict of interests is so vivid that it is difficult to count on a quick
and constructive compromise. The whole problem, however, comes
down to a juxtaposition of lobbying forces – rich and poor countries
and corporations occupying different positions in global value chains,

the best example of which are the final provisions of the Agreement on Trade-Related Aspects of Intellectual Property Rights (TRIPS), which were achieved after considerable compromises.

When analysing numerous patented inventions – especially in the area of software – it would be difficult to indicate that they have even met the relatively low requirement of obviousness. In many cases, the obviousness is striking even for people outside the industry, and even more so for the 'expert' referred to in the binding regulations, who is to be the point of reference. The patented double-click of the computer mouse may serve as the best example (US patent 7,171,625).

In the face of ever faster technological advancement, the best solution would ultimately be to indicate that patents are granted only for such inventions that significantly contribute to the development of the current state of the art. Notwithstanding that, however, even a moderately restrictive understanding of the requirement of non-obviousness would significantly contribute to curbing patent flooding. A 'finer sieve' applied by Patent Offices would not admit mock patents, the existence of which cannot be reconciled with the standard grounds and reasons for legal protection of inventions. On the other hand, the emergence of such exclusive rights is a breeding ground for blackmailers – patent trolls – and creates a thicket that hinders smaller companies from entering the market. Moreover, current patent flooding means that the cost of searching patent databases (at the stage of verifying the patent purity) is substantial even for larger companies. Some claim that even when this procedure is done diligently, it may still not guarantee a sufficient level of legal protection (which is also accounted for by the circumstances described below).

2.1.2 Patent racing

Another issue that affects the low average quality of patents is the need to apply for a patent at a very early stage of project development, which is a derivative of the patent racing based on the 'winner takes all' principle. Furthermore, larger companies patent many constructs on a 'just in case' basis. Given a certain scale of operations, the costs of obtaining a patent are relatively low and managers are more afraid of closing a product development path than of costs sunk in patenting procedures. When adopting such a strategy, those companies become similar to patent trolls in terms of their approach, for they develop intellectual property not for the purpose of commercial operations.

As a result, the average quality of patents is low. Breakthrough constructs are lost in the maze of pseudo-inventions with virtually zero commercial potential. As one of the studies indicates (Elkin-Koren & Salzberger, 2013, p. 94), the vast majority of patents have never been the subject of a court dispute – only 1.5%, out of which only 0.1% of cases have been brought to a court trial. On the other hand, 46% of patents have been annulled under enforceable court decisions. It means that the current state of affairs may be described by means of the arms race metaphor mentioned in the previous chapter: most of the arsenal created has never been in use (and has never been intended to be used) but has been merely accumulated to deter opponents. And when the real potential has been challenged, it often turns out that they are dummies or misfires.

As mentioned earlier, patent racing forces one to promptly file inventions with Patent Offices, since they almost exclusively work on the basis of the 'first to file' principle, not the 'first to invent' principle. It means that the decision to patent must be taken at a very early stage of the innovation process. It forces costs to be incurred (and in the long run contributes to the creation of patent thickets) even before the emergence of a clear idea of how to commercialise a given invention (Lemley & Shapiro, 2005, p. 77). It is worthwhile to compare this information with data quoted by (Elkin-Koren & Salzberger, 2013, p. 94), where the costs of filing a patent with the American Patent Office (including legal services and other fees) range between $10,000 and $30,000, while the possible costs of court proceedings are over $1,500,000 per each party.

The largest systemic problem arising from the phenomenon of patent racing is the duplication of research, which means that the capital expenditure incurred by all economic entities, except for the one that has obtained the patent, must be counted as sunk costs. It is the price payable for research acceleration. It is difficult to expect even a comparatively high pace of research if it weren't for the aforementioned competitive mechanisms. It does not mean, however, that active national policy cannot partially alleviate the above-mentioned drawbacks.

2.1.3 Functional claims

Still another problem in this category is the fact that Patent Offices accept ambiguous patent claims, i.e. the reading of which is insufficient to allow a professionally eligible person to duplicate the construct. It contradicts the conceptual framework of the intellectual property law which accepts social inconveniences arising from the monopoly in exchange for the dissemination of the construct. As a result, collections of patents do not play an educational role that could inspire subsequent inventors to make further innovations.

Furthermore, the policy of various contemporary companies paradoxically aims at prohibiting the search for patent claims belonging to competitors (sic!). The point is that, on the one hand, engineers should not be inspired by constructs, the applicability of which may be doubtful. On the other hand, in the case of a lawsuit, this is to make it difficult to demonstrate deliberate patent infringement, which in certain legal regimes would give a chance to obtain three times the average compensation (Boldrin & Levine, 2013, p. 10).

The immanent features of intellectual property are its blurry boundaries. However, in the case of low quality patents, the uncertainty space is extremely large. From the point of view of innovation, this phenomenon is doubly dangerous. First of all, because the ambiguous description of the patented invention does not contribute sufficiently to the development of society's knowledge, although it may, after all, expect the inventor to reveal something valuable and improvable and freely useable after the patent expires, in exchange for a legal monopoly. Second, it is a much stronger barrier for other players to enter the market. A vague patent hampers the phenomenon of inventing around the patent (because the area under protection is imprecise). Any litigation may therefore be particularly unpredictable in such circumstances. As a result, although such patents do not carry a high market value, they indirectly provide for development of significant competitive advantages. However, it is performed in a manner that is not acceptable from the social point of view.

Such particular examples of vague patents are those based on functional claims. It comes down to the issue of the admissibility of patenting constructs that are characterised by a high degree of abstraction, and their translation into specific technical arrangements is purely theoretical. In particular, software patent lawyers are increasingly filing patent claims in such a broad, functional manner. In fact, patenters then do not demand a legal monopoly on a specific device or even a sequence of steps to achieve a goal, but on the purpose (intent) itself (Lemley, 2012, p. 905).

The provisions of the patent law do not explicitly require a patent claim to be free from functional features. The technical features specified in the claim should, however, distinguish the claimed invention from other constructs. It is therefore indisputable that the strict scope of the features cannot be doubted. The wide use of functional terms, which occurs in the case of software, means that a given patent protects a huge area of technology, even if it has not been tested and actually developed by the applicant.

In general, the patent claims that define the invention by the effect to be achieved should be inadmissible, especially if they relate only to the underlying technical problem. However, functional reservations may be admissible if the invention may only be defined in this way or it cannot be defined more precisely without excessive restriction on the scope of the reservations (Sichelman, 2010, p. 350).

Due to the nature of software, such situation is relatively rare in this field. Much more often it is simply a matter of patenting the widest possible area, even if as a result its boundaries will be difficult to determine precisely. The fulfilment of the above-mentioned conditions is therefore possible in completely different branches of industry. Moreover, the absurdity of broad functional patenting may be seen especially when the mechanism is transferred to other industries. Hence, in the pharmaceutical industry, it would signify the possibility of reserving 'such an arrangement of atoms that cures cancer', which would let a case be brought to court against any other company that will develop a specific construct to achieve such a goal (Lemley, 2012, p. 908).

The tragedy of such constructs also results from the fact that they contradict the foundation and ground for legal protection of inventions. They completely disrupt the relationship between the awarded privilege-monopoly (associated with social inconvenience) and the scope of disclosed information (which is to compensate for it) (Graham & Vishnubhakat, 2013, p. 81). It is hardly surprising that such practices have greatly contributed to the emergence of the Tragedy of Intangible Abundance.

2.1.4 Software patents

The aforementioned software sector deserves to be called a separate (fourth) component of the problem described in this section, which is the low average quality of patents. Moreover, it bears noting that the controversy related to software patenting underlies the major arguments for the liberalisation of the industrial property law (Bessen & Meurer, 2008, p. 187). In some instances, patenting weaknesses and its irrationality are believed to be most visible in the case of software. Of course, it would be hard to imagine the complete abandonment of patenting software since it is an essentially significant factor in terms of occurring innovation. Furthermore, it is strongly correlated with non-software-derived inventions and it would be hard to precisely set the patent zone boundaries.

A number of authors (e.g. Cambell-Kelly, 2005; Lemley, 2012; Mann, 2005; Miller, 2014) recognise numerous drawbacks of software patents. The very phenomenon of software patenting is comparatively novel. Software initially could not be incorporated into the definition of patentability within the meaning of classic interpretation of legal regulations. In the United States the number of software patents started to grow exponentially in the mid-1990s. Within this context, in terms of the American law it is significant that on 26th of May 1981 Attorney Satya Pal Asija received a patent for a computer software program called Swift-answer (though one must bear in mind that the first patent protection of that kind was granted in Great Britain in 1966). Generally, software patentability is regarded as much more widespread in the United States than in Europe.

The analysis of conditions leading to software patent dysfunction indicates the sizeable adversities faced by the open source software movement founders (who expose themselves to possible lawsuits after having disclosed source codes) as well as the growing risk of creating more complex projects (operating systems, for instance) based on thousands of potentially patented constructs.

Those inconveniences arise from some of the aforementioned causes of the Tragedy of Intangible Abundance, mainly growing patent thickets or patent trolls and the activities they undertake. However, we can identify three original core causes of problems with software patenting:

1 No need to patent the software, as the software source code is protected by copyright law and related regulations; therefore, if the primary protection goal is not pursued in that case, the void is filled with activities aimed at taking advantage of patents in contravention of their social and economic purpose (for instance, in the case of arms race)
2 The aforementioned extremely liberal approach to the requirement of non-obviousness (that is particularly risky in the case of software that often lacks physical emanation), which has led to patent flooding
3 Approval of functional claims has made patent boundaries even more blurred.

It also bears noting that at the very beginning the software industry represented far-reaching scepticism in respect of that form of protection of intellectual property. In the following years it became a regular occurrence that the majority of software patents were not filed by strictly software companies but by companies from the much wider sphere of IT. Those facts make it plausible to conclude that software patents do not yield net benefits for that industry but, due to a multitude of court cases, primarily bring about high social costs (Bessen, 2011, pp. 2–3). Moreover, as S. P. Miller noticed (Miller, 2014, p. 838) there is strong empirical evidence that software patents have caused the quality of the whole patenting system to substantially degrade.

For the strictly software industry, software patents are less effective than for enterprises operating in other branches of industry. For a number of software creators, copyright law provides sufficient protection and motivation to work. Due to the fact that software patents were not needed to assure any system of incentives to invent and publicise the related deliverables, a space appeared for utilising them for alternative purposes. Therefore they are most often used for developing patent portfolios that are to be advantageous in negotiations within the context of cross-licensing, lawsuit risk mitigation, or simply to block new market entrants (Bessen & Hunt, 2007, p. 184). Such enterprises do not use patents for their primary commercial purposes. Escalation of the aforementioned categories of activities undoubtedly accounts for the deformation of the system of patent-based protection for inventions.

The aim to ensure the effective research and development incentive has underlain the implementation of the patent protection and its maintenance in consecutive centuries. Research assessing the impact of software patents upon R&D in respective companies has, however, indicated the number of software patents grew in relation to the number of other patents obtained by a company, while R&D expenses fell (Bessen, 2011, p. 8). Additionally, no confirmation was found for the arguments from software patenting supporters that such protection raised the rate of return on public investments such as university research grants, and facilitated knowledge transfer.

In other industries patents are also used for purposes other than those underlying the motives of invention protection. However, in the case of software patenting that dissonance is exceptionally overwhelming. In the software domain it is particularly difficult to define whether the requirement of non-obviousness has been satisfied since the filed inventions lack a physical emanation. For that reason it initially was extremely difficult to prove the evident non-obviousness of a source code. The problem is that non-restrictive observance of that requirement – in order to ensure any viability of software patenting – no longer prevents banal constructs from being patented. Consequently such functionalities that are really obvious not only for a professional but also for individuals with moderately expanded knowledge on a given sector of industry become patentable. That may be exemplified by the most basic functionalities of an online store depicted on the website: https://webshop.ffii.org (for instance: Electronic shopping cart – EP807891, Tabbed palettes and restrict search: EP689133 and EP1131752, Preview window: EP537100).

2.2 Patent flooding

Low quality of patents is correlated with the huge number of patents (Graph 2.1). For that reason, the related literature (Bessen & Meurer, 2008, p. 11) makes reference to flood patenting.

A closer look at the causes of patent flooding proves China to be the major source of it and the United States to a smaller extent (Graph 2.2). From the perspective of the 1990s, inclusion of China into the global system of intellectual property protection seemed to

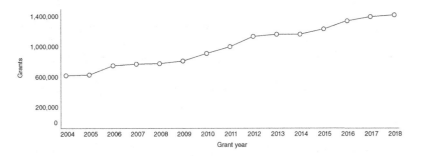

Graph 2.1 Patents granted worldwide, 2001–2017.
Source: WIPO (2018, p. 31).

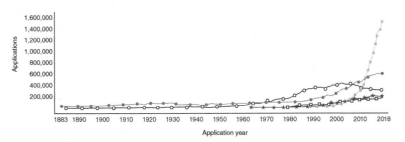

Graph 2.2 Trend in patent applications for the top five offices, 1883–2017.
Source: WPIO (p. 26).

be a great challenge, necessary to sustain globalisation (Li, 2019). The way in which it has been accomplished is somewhat a caricature. Formal implementation of global standards of intellectual property protection safeguards the global corporations against Asian fakes to a small extent. Furthermore, the enormous number of patent claims from that territory (that is often geographically extended onto other markets) has significantly given rise to the Tragedy of Intangible Abundance.

2.2.1 Focus on legal monopolies

Apart from the aforementioned global conditions, the micro-scale must be taken into account in the form of decisions made by specific enterprises. In many of them, intangible resources management based on legal monopolies is the default approach and may be seen as the only one available. So, the dominant conceptual framework is one of patenting any intellectual property that has been developed to be used in a product (larger companies even aim to patent whatever may possibly be used in the manufacturing process). Often, no attempt is made to estimate the costs and benefits of using alternative methods such as trade secrets, defensive publishing, or 'pay what you want' systems.

This state of affairs originates from the conviction that legal monopolies allow to increase the earnings yielded by the innovator (Boldrin & Levine, 2008, p. 150). However, the cost that must be incurred on such protection is forgotten. The costs are much in excess of fees payable to a patent office, although when we factor in the number of countries where protection is required, the cost value cannot be ignored even in the case of larger companies. A major issue is the fact that only a minor number of patents are useful for an organisation.

An often ignored cost is the need to precisely describe an invention in the patent application form that is subject to disclosure. It means providing imitators with ready-made constructs and easier discoveries around the patent, and in the case of countries where intellectual property rights are enforced less effectively, it leads to unauthorised use of an invention. The scale of that problem varies depending on the sector of economy and geographical area.

Supporters of monopolistic arrangements argue with conviction that in case of unlimited accessibility perfect competition will force the price down to nearly the level of marginal cost and thus will not only prevent collecting the innovation bonus but even deny recovering the costs incurred in this activity

The following counter-arguments challenge the above approach:

1   Price may possibly approximate to the marginal cost value but in the mid or long term, which is less and less significant, given the shortening product life cycle.
2   The above implication disregards the fact that while the very idea (pure intellectual property) is not uncommon the production assets indispensable for delivery of a ready-made product that incorporates intellectual property are subject to all the limitations imminent in the traditional economy.
3   Due to the emergence of natural monopolies, the marginal cost value will not be the same for all manufacturers. In numerous cases it is the innovator (inter alia in result of time advantage) who is the most predisposed to building a sustainably large scale of operations enabling the greatest possible reduction of the marginal cost – unachievable for the market players that will become competitors with a delay.

Within this context J. Stiglitz points out that a monopoly cannot be temporary (contrary to what Schumpeter has argued) (Stiglitz, 2008, p. 1705). Due to the networking effect as well as high switching costs (in terms of products and services), the monopoly that has been once set is hard to challenge. It may be exemplified by Microsoft, the current dominant position of which arises, to a great extent, from legal monopolies that became extinct long ago. That mechanism – of creating standards and the networking effect – may, however, be successfully exploited regardless of legal monopolies, which is elaborated upon in the subsequent part of the book.

2.2.2 *Innovativeness pressure with patents as output indicators*

The aforementioned indefinability of intangible resources results in excessive value being assigned to intangible assets that may be recognised in the standard balance sheet of an enterprise. It is particularly visible in the area of intellectual property that may be protected by means of copyright law or industrial property law. Consequently, the instruments derived from legal monopolies become the dominant intellectual property management tools in enterprises. (Biga, 2017, pp. 150–151).

This fits into a larger problem of assessing innovativeness of economies/ sectors / enterprises / staff members through the prism of the number of patents received. T. Geodecki elaborates upon the problems with such innovativeness indicators (Geodecki, 2008). If R&D expenses and labour cost are not the best innovativeness indicators in that sector of economy, high-tech and patent indicators in terms of research outcomes will obviously copy the R&D-related drawbacks. Patents are rather invention indicators instead of innovation indicators, thus they namely evidence technological novelty (novel technique) but not marketable innovation. As a result, patent indicators may disregard numerous innovations that are different from invention or many inventions and technologies that are not patentable or those that still arouse serious doubts in terms of possible patentability (for instance, human DNA strands). The comparison of the patenting rate and innovativeness indicators highlights the errors that may arise from the innovativeness analysis based on a patent indicator. T. Geodecki (2008, p. 44) points to:

1   Underestimated innovation-oriented activities in the sectors with lower technological opportunities.
2   Overestimated innovation-oriented activities in enterprises cooperating in R&D that prefer to patent the most precious knowledge prior to cooperation commencement.
3   Underestimated scale of innovation-oriented activities in small-sized enterprises for which the cost of the whole procedure is too high.
4   Overestimated innovation-oriented activities in small-sized enterprises that already own a patent (the trend to patent a larger number of constructs due to costs already incurred).

Innovativeness pressure, understood as the number of patents awarded, was conceived primarily by two groups of professionals: scientists and managers. For the former patent as a measure is very comfortable due to data accessibility. Patent Offices maintain open registers that, in liaison with other databases (Orbis, Amadeus), allow to analyse data in diverse contexts: a sector of economy, company size, a type of business, shareholding structure, etc., which is very useful in terms of economic research.

In literature (Stiglitz, 2008) it is emphasised that pursuing legal monopolies is not the only strategy that allows for effective utilisation of intellectual property developed within the enterprise. It is also indicated that due to the growing awareness of legal protection deficiencies, in many industries alternative methods of intangible resources management are exploited to a greater extent (Bessen & Meurer, 2008). As a result, more and more companies refuse to regard easy copying, which is the immanent feature of intellectual property solely as a threat. Rather, they perceive it as an opportunity to accelerate the emergence of a new market, expand marketability of complementary goods and services, or take advantage of business models that are founded upon the networking effect. Then, although their strategies happen to be more effective, in terms of innovativeness indicators they lose out to competitors that rely on standard strategies.

The above conditions mean that in economic analysis of the intellectual property law it is extremely hard to compare respective countries. Additional factors must be added: (1) varied entry barriers other than legal monopolies, (2) non-uniform engagement of countries in supporting open innovations, and (3) differentiated effectiveness of enforcement of intellectual property rights in result of court proceedings. In the most restrictive systems, for instance in Japan, patents are the most effective tools. However, the studies conducted in the United States (Lallement, 2017) as well as the data compiled in the Community Innovation Survey (CIS) indicate that in other parts of the world informal methods are much more profitable (time advantage, trade secrets, comprehensiveness of products). Company size or innovation development status may be other significant factors that account for the extent to which legal measures are applied. In the context of global value chains, some authors (Lea, 2008) even suggest that intellectual property rights constitute a tax paid by developing countries.

As far as managers are concerned, their reports are based on registered exclusive rights as objective and universal due to the problems related with recognition, indicators, and valuation of intangible assets. They often highlight patent-related information, being aware of the affirmation for intangible resources in business. Due to the lack of satisfactory indicators or valuation methods (elaborated upon in the following subchapter), it is the only way to justify incurring research and development costs that are often high.

That is, however, a vicious circle. Specific staff members are often assessed in terms of the number of submitted patents. From their point of view, there is no incentive to pursue alternative methods of managing some of the intangible resources. Moreover, in the prevailing incentive system, any bonus is not principally correlated with any real economic benefits arising from a patent that a company may earn. So, for an employee the effectiveness of resource utilisation does not matter at all, neither does the amount of sunk costs incurred on registration of redundant patents.

Thus, not only lawyers and economists prove to be excessively inclined towards intellectual property management founded on

obtained legal monopolies. Managers, staff members, and researchers also display inclination to abuse patenting in accordance with
individual rationality. That problem will neither be addressed by the
pressure from investors who are also strongly attached to a patent
being a 'tangible' proof of innovativeness proof, that they must be satisfied with, given the lack of other credible sources of reporting.

2.3 Immeasurable intangible resources

In the knowledge-based economy, measurement or assessment and
valuation of intangible resources could seemingly be so important
that development of precise and transferable methods is just a matter
of time. In reality, however, the multiplicity of methods is still hardly
sufficient. Most of all, there are no precise answers to the question
what the purpose of such a quasi-universal system could be. What
could be its primary objective? What could be the motivation underlying credible reporting (Hunter, Webster, & Wyatt, 2005, p. 63)?

For tax purposes, accounting is the most topical issue within the
framework of companies' external relations. Within this context,
intangible resources, that have been booked reliably, would most of
all serve the purpose of tax optimisation. Given that implication,
however, such assessment and valuation will not have any practical
usefulness in terms of a company's management and pro-development
thinking. Furthermore, that kind of reporting will be less and less
useful for investors, which is also the case with tax accounting of
intangible assets. In that sense it is a mere attempt to minimise tax
payables instead of reflecting the real financial standing and potential
of an enterprise in a reliable manner.

That problem cannot be so easily addressed by separate reporting
oriented on the internal needs of an enterprise. In that case misrep-
resentations will arise from manipulating results within the organisational hierarchy. Subordinates will most often bend reality in order to
report the highest possible growth of intangible resources to receive
a better evaluation. It may be extremely dangerous when patents and
other legal monopolies are commonly regarded as primary innovation
indicators. It may exert stronger pressure on thoughtless patenting.

The best approach could seem to be the development of rigid and
precise assessment and valuation guidelines. However, that is extremely
difficult. Given the contemporary background knowledge, it even
seems to be impossible to achieve, especially in the form of standards
that would be commonly acceptable, usable, and would consequently
allow to benchmarking enterprises. It is currently more viable to merely

create internal systems for specific companies (possibly for capital groups). They could be founded on some of the numerous commonly acceptable and used methods that would only have to be adjusted to the business profile of a company. The aforementioned tools would have to be most of all adapted to a company's strategy in order to develop such a system, since a strategy sets out the time horizon, expected deliverables, verification and up-dating methods, etc.

There is no sufficient systemic motivation to create an intellectual capital reporting system that could be regarded as universal. That obviously leads to information asymmetry and subjective market valuation of a company that may induce disruptive capital flows. From a broader perspective, it will simply bring about ineffective allocation of investment assets (Sebastian, Dumitrascu, & Pele, 2017).

According to M. Wasilewska –

> such a policy may result in inefficient allocation of assets that are invested in innovative companies (for instance, Internet companies), notwithstanding the investments that are hardly rooted in the value of such companies. Such investments bring about more extensive fluctuation in the market, changing market rates, which directly results from the lack of objective information on intangible assets. On the other hand, valuation of intangible resources based on acquisition costs does not always make sense since it is correlated with its value to a lesser extent than in the case of tangible assets. Another concern is the fact that many managers would not be willing to reveal detailed information on intangible resources because they often are strategic resources of a company and are protected against competition. Valuation of intangible assets would also be problematic in terms of information benchmarking within one company.
>
> (Wasilewska, 2015, p. 62)

Threats and opportunities that arise from intellectual capital valuation and reporting are displayed in Table 2.1.

2.3.1 Purpose-related concerns

Objective difficulties in accounting of intangible resources must be taken into account (Oleksak & Adams, 2010, p. 94). The primary difficulty is that the majority of them (for instance, staff members or relations) are not in possession of an enterprise while the accounting system aims to identify all that is under control of an enterprise.

Table 2.1 Threats and Opportunities Arising from Intellectual Capital Valuation and Reporting

Opportunities	*Threats*
1 Solid grounds for company valuation.	1 Intangible resources are too risky and tentative to be recognised as assets in the accounting books.
2 Managers focused on critical factors, long-range vision driven by better communication, intellectual capital indicators may measure the strategy implementation deliverables.	
3 Reasoned investment in knowledge management.	2 Depreciation of intangible resources could lead to abuse and manipulation.
4 Lower cost of capital, higher share/stock price.	
5 Opportunity to measure the strategy implementation progress and performance output indicators.	3 Acquisition cost of intangible resources will correspond to the related valuation to much lesser extent than in the case of tangible assets.
6 Opportunity to use the deliverables for the purpose of the staff incentive scheme, particularly managers.	
7 Human resources management and customer relations facilitator.	4 Failure of investment projects in liaison with intangible resources recognised in the balance sheet could lead to litigation.
8 Sustainability of development and awareness of business operations amongst groups of interest.	
9 Improvement of communication with external stakeholders (disclosure of information on real value of a company and forecast earnings).	5 Many managers would not like to disclose details regarding intangible resources.
10 Improvement of transparency of business operations and mitigation of information asymmetry and related quality improvement of information disclosed to stockholders.	6 Problematic information benchmarking, given the diverse business profiles.
11 Obtaining additional information that may be useful in decision making.	7 Lack of uniform intellectual capital reporting standards.
12 Valuation of intangible assets may help the enterprise to raise funds.	
13 Reasons and grounds for high licence fees payable by foreign subsidies to the head office, when questioned by tax authorities.	8 Information on intellectual capital could be used by competition.
14 Enhanced transparency of information published by an enterprise.	
15 Building trust among staff members and other key stakeholders.	

Source: Wasilewska (2015, p. 63).

Second, the value of intangible resources is strictly correlated with other interrelated resources. It is therefore difficult to separate human resources from relations or structural capital. Third, they are extremely hard to valuate based on transactions (that is one of primary valuation methods), since they are made relatively rarely in the case of intangible resources.

However, it must be explicitly underlined that the purpose of assessment and valuation of intangible resources may give rise to related concerns. From the perspective of long-term enterprise development, the most important aims – the recognition of true value of a company or detailed identification of its competitive advantage – may be overshadowed by other incentives that are very often operational. Moreover, some of them contradict one another to a great extent, which further intensifies chaos in that respect.

The tax-oriented approach dominates in the case of companies that do not pay much attention to intangible resources management. Within this context, assessment and valuation of intangible resources is to most of all serve the purpose of the aforementioned tax minimisation. The term 'innovativeness' is often used for benefiting from substantial tax incentives. The government is also subject to innovativeness-driven pressure and is willing to provide innovative entrepreneurs with preferential terms and conditions. The systemic support for improvement of economic competitiveness by means of awarding bonuses to entrepreneurs that invest in research and development is obviously purposeful, particularly within the context of counteracting the middle income trap. In the economy of marginal costs approximating to zero (Rifkin, 2014), it is really hard to successfully compete in the long run through traditional means such as cheap labour or energy resources. The level of innovativeness of products and services is increasingly crucial.

The problem is that the innovativeness focus is too often correlated with indicators based on registered exclusive rights and state aid that is vague, which encourages entrepreneurs to take advantage of the peculiar form of creative reporting. Such activities do not translate into expected innovativeness but only intensify the reporting chaos. In consequence, assessment and valuation of intangible resources done in such conditions just obscure the whole picture. Furthermore, they hamper independent and parallel reporting for internal purposes in fear of possible juxtaposition of official and unofficial documents that could unveil superficial reporting for tax purposes and bring about the risk of significant financial consequences.

2.3.2 *Deficiency of tools*

Benchmarking may be a challenge mostly due to the lack of unified standards for reporting of intangible resources as well as common assessment and valuation methods applicable to respective intangible assets (Oleksak & Adams, 2010). The most commonly acceptable market-based valuation allows to valuate only a minor part of intangible resources, namely the one that has served the transaction purpose. The other valuation methods – option-based, cost-based, earnings-based valuation – incorporate too many arbitrary, non-standard factors.

The scale of granted licences may to some extent account for patent strength (respective companies, sectors of economy, countries). The related literature has referred to the efforts undertaken to assess the scale of licensing (Alikhan, Mashelkar, & Martinez, 2006). However, they have been grounded on fairly superficial high-level data. Patent pooling and cross-licensing are additionally difficult to be accounted for. They are not reliably reflected in enterprises' financial statements, and they are crucial for a number of sectors of economy (mainly IT). Standardisation organisations that enforce licensing in conformity with FRAND requirements also distort the valuation outcome (Shapiro, 2001).

The OECD originally defined intangible assets to include all investments aiming at increasing future earnings as a result of activities other than acquisition of fixed assets [OECD, 1992, s. 114]. The subsequent OECD Report made in 2000 with more precision defined intangible assets to be capital expenditures on all new, target-oriented measures or tools used in an enterprise for the purpose of increasing the quantity or expanding the background knowledge or acquiring or improving the existing assets or intended for acquiring utterly new knowledge (Skrzypek, 2014, p. 97).

According to A. Bounfour (Bounfour, 2003), data accessibility is the basic problem. Not only is there a lack of data but it is very difficult to compile relevantly long data sequences. Data benchmarking is also problematic due to varied data sources. Limited data accessibility makes any data benchmarking (among countries, industries, companies) extremely difficult – more so as the most valuable conclusions may be arrived at only after multidimensional analyses. Even the R&D investment ratio that has been applied for a long time now is questionable since it is distorted by fiscal innovation-oriented incentives that account for considerable discrepancies between the substance-based innovation evidence and its formal rendition.

A. Bounfour (2003, p. 46) draws attention that the R&D debate focuses on the data compiled from the production sector, which only represents some part of economic reality. Moreover, the more the economy is based on knowledge and moves into the digital world, the less representative the related figures become. Each of the intangible resources valuation methods has drawbacks that make depending on their results unreliable (Table 2.2 displays the details).

Table 2.2 Strengths and Weaknesses of Intangible Resources Valuation Methods

Method	Strengths	Weaknesses
Market value minus book value	Simple applicability, quick, relatively easy access to data, interpretability, comparability, most commonly used for pricing the initial value of intellectual capital.	Founded on extensive simplification, should be treated mainly as a point of reference for further analyses, inaccurately reflects complexity of reality, numerator and denominator are derived from two different computation procedures.
Tobin's Q	Commonly applied, the ratio is easily computable accessible data, the ratio is easily interpretable and comprehensible, provides for benchmarking. It mitigates some of the adverse impact of the MV-BV method in effect of replacing book value with replacement value, considered to be better.	Too simplified a definition of intellectual capital. Replacement cost is sometimes difficult to estimate, which affects practicability of the ratio. Furthermore, that ratio is subject to the same exogenous variables due to the fact that the numerator is notoriously subject to unforeseeable fluctuations, which do not often have much in common with the real company's value.
Value Added Intellectual Coefficient (VAIC)	Simple computation and the data is available in annual financial statements that are thus objective and verifiable.	Overly extensive simplification of pricing the intellectual capital, the value of human capital equivalent to the labour cost causes the value of the intellectual capital to be underestimated as compared to the other methods. Some empirical studies are disappointing in terms of the VAIC accountable for the company's performance output indicators

(Continued)

Method	Strengths	Weaknesses
Knowledge Capital Earnings	It is a logical method that is commonly acceptable in terms of the intellectual capital valuation all over the world, data is accessible and verifiable, the method allows for benchmarking among sectors of economy, time series analyses. Empirical studies confirm relevancy of that method for the purpose of investment decision making as there is a strong correlation between the rate of return for the stock and the rate of return on the intellectual capital.	The need to conduct in-depth studies and calculations in terms of the specific conditionalities of the economy under study. That method is to define one aggregated value of the intellectual capital, disregarding the value of its respective components, which is useful for external reporting purposes but does not provide for evaluation of management of respective components of the intellectual capital.
Calculated Intangible Value	It is a very interesting method that is often regarded as one of the best methods to reflect the intellectual capital in enterprises, that is founded on logical, objective, and reliable valuation, data is accessible, comparable.	The method is fairly labour-intensive, and in order for it to be applicable, the ROA of an enterprise must be in excess of the average value for the sector as a whole. The lower ratio results in the negative values that are not logical. It uses average values that are often inaccurate.

Source: Fijałkowska (2012, pp. 422–423).

Data deficiency arises from the fact that data compiling/processing for the purpose of the primary objective is useless from the scientific point of view, apart from the immanently seemingly immeasurable intangible resources. The attempts to report as high as possible values of intangible assets in order to create the image of a modern company being awarded bonuses or benefiting from tax incentives end up with overestimation of those resources.

2.4 Propertisation of intangible assets

Some authors draw attention to the error of intangible resources-related discussion increasingly focusing on ownership rights and the free-rider problem. In the economic theory of ownership, the emphasis is put on the mitigation of the adverse impact of externalities, which are usually negative in nature. It is also basically a zero-sum game in which one's benefit (even in the case of a free rider) must mean the loss incurred by someone who cannot use a resource (which may be problematic, especially when someone shared the resource acquisition costs, contrary to a free rider).

M. Lemley (2004, p. 1044) also underlines that 'propertisation' of intellectual resources is a relatively new phenomenon. Such ownership-centric approach was not originally noticeable. The cited author has analysed the usage of the term 'intellectual property' in the jurisdiction exercised by federal courts in consecutive decades (Table 2.3).

The career of that term may be explained by the attempt to build one's self-esteem in the case of individuals creating this kind of resources when they were not so much appreciated as nowadays. In consequence, all the ownership connotations were incorporated into the mainstream, which contributed to the occurrence of the Tragedy of Intangible Abundance. Consideration of intangible resources in terms of ownership was popularised not only among judges, and became common in the legal profession, but also among economists and managers. However, accountants seem to have faced (still face) major

Table 2.3 Number of the References Made to 'Intellectual Property' in the Jurisdiction Exercised by Federal Courts

Years	Number of references made to 'Intellectual Property'
1993–2003	3,863
1983–1993	1,510
1973–1983	555
1963–1973	327
1953–1963	303
1943–1953	201

Source: Lemley (2004, p. 1044).

problems with the recognition of intangible resources in terms of ownership or property. In their rigid framework, it is difficult to account for something that is nonphysical and uncontrollable.

2.4.1 Differentiation from tangible assets

In the era of growing importance of intellectual property, it is extremely significant to answer the question whether deliberations on classically understood 'property' may be – and if yes, to what extent – extrapolated to intellectual property. Superficial analysis as well as linguistic issues account for regarding intellectual property as one kind of property – as if intellectual property were included in the set of ownership rights. However those notions differ substantially, while linguistic analysis is misleading since the relation between ownership and intellectual property is rather an independence relation, i.e. in some aspects intellectual property displays features pertaining to ownership – it performs like property but in other aspects it is totally different or even contrary in nature.

Patent may be considered in terms of ownership or quasi-ownership exclusively when property is perceived in a totally new manner. It is in opposition to the former understanding in which ownership is perceived in the context of facilities and relations between them and people whereas an ownership right – as possession, usage, and power of disposal. The novel understanding defines ownership to be the power to control.

The conceptual frameworks developed by J. Lock and J. Bentham have been critical in shaping the content of the abstract notion that ownership is. The former regarded ownership as God's gift and the latter – in the context of being that exists in result of the decision of the authorities and as such should be protected by them, which incorporates itself into the conviction that a state should rationally shape social relations, and interpersonal relations should be created in such a way that will allow for ethics to be enforced (it is feasible exclusively when private property is respected). Due to the connotations between the economic analysis of law and utilitarianism, the further elaborations are grounded on the conceptual framework by J. Bentham (Biga, 2017, pp. 18–19).

It also needs to be underlined that the issue of ownership rights is one of the topical issues in the debate on economic development and economic efficiency. Discussions on common-pool resources are particularly intensive since excessive exploitation of common-pool resources causes efficiency to fall and in extreme cases it is even threatened with damaging a source of resources. The extent of boundaries of private property is the problem that is most vivid in that respect.

Fundamental differences between tangible assets and intellectual property are:

1   Scarcity of goods
2   Notification
3   Imprecise nature of boundaries
4   High risk and unpredictability of litigation

2.4.1.1 *Scarcity of goods*

The majority of justifications underlying the existence of property and its protection arise from the fact that goods – within the traditional meaning – are scarce and as such cannot be used by an unlimited number of people. Intangible assets, including inventions (understood as intellectual creation and not as a specific machine or an amount of substance), may be used by an unlimited number of people without any prejudice to other individuals. A patent owner, granting a licence, provides a licensee with the same functionality regardless of the number of licences granted. The economic potential of respective licences will obviously shrink with the growing number of those entitled to use an invention for commercial purposes. Moreover, the same invention may be concurrently created by two totally independent researchers. Such a case is just out of question in respect of a conventional property (Biga, 2017, p. 23).

2.4.1.2 *Notification*

In the case of a tangible asset it is relatively easy to manifest one's ownership. Moreover, competent authorities maintain relevant registers in respect of real estate or vehicles that are of utmost importance for commercial transactions. The case with intangible assets is totally different, which is one of the basic deficiencies in the legal system of invention protection. There are patent databases. However, their usability is much less extensive (than in the case of land registries and requires much longer analyses linked with the need to put risky interpretations. Investors cannot be guaranteed that even extensive studies on the state of technology carried out by means of analysing patents that have been granted will not prevent them from the infringement of one's exclusive right.

2.4.1.3 Imprecise nature of boundaries

Another issue is the ambiguity of intellectual property boundaries. It very rarely applies to tangible assets (e.g. disputes in respect of geodetic activities, conflicts resulting from discrepancies in the portioning of office space). In majority of tangible assets, their boundaries are set by the physical properties – there are no doubts about the end of a laptop or a vehicle. In the case of increasing vagueness of patent claims, the boundaries are becoming more and more ambiguous. It is a similar case with other categories of intellectual property – design, copyright. It is hard to precisely declare where the act of plagiarising or another form of infringement begins. Some researchers represent a harsh perspective in that respect: if you are not able to define its boundaries precisely, it is not a property (Bessen & Meurer, 2008, p. 9).

2.4.1.4 High risk and unpredictability of litigation

The above-mentioned peculiarities of intellectual property come forward with the necessity to face a totally different scale of infringement, and in consequence much higher costs of litigations arising mainly from their unpredictability. Effectiveness of legal measures of intellectual property protection may be proven mainly by court statistics (Allison, Lamley, & Schwartz, 2015), including the percentage of court cases won by patent holders. In the case of pharmaceutical patents it is 57.8%, mechanical patents – 54%, and software patents – 40.2%, and biotechnology patents – only 32%, which allows us to conclude that 'a patent quality is tailored to the industry'. That issue is elaborated upon in the subsequent chapter on symptoms of the Tragedy of Intangible Abundance.

The positive nature of intellectual property externalities is easily noticeable. It is totally contrary to the situation that economists became accustomed to in connection with tangible assets where, as a rule, companies attempt to abdicate their responsibility for adverse impact of their business operations – for instance, some companies claim to contaminate the natural environment in the name of operational efficiency improvement.

The issue of externalities cannot be exclusively limited to their negative impacts. For example, a unique composition of flowers in front of a house or a mural on a wall causes some benefits derived from landscape enhancement to be enjoyed by third parties who will see the flowerbed or the painted mural. From the social point of view, there is no need to undertake the effort to mitigate the impact of such externalities. In the interest of the very creator, it would be obvious to earn benefits from performed work, which is achievable by means of royalties to some extent.

This notion helps to comprehend the irrationality of intellectual property law and related regulations. Mitigation of the impact of externalities cannot underlie the law that is enforced. It neither can be the argument for a stricter regime. In the case of intellectual property, mainly positive externalities are the outcome. In that case, the institutional framework that is to facilitate internalisation of externalities is in itself counterproductive. Therefore, M. Lemley (2004, p. 1044) recommends the departure from the traditional theory of property towards utilitarianism, which notwithstanding substantial limitations allows to approximate the balance between boundaries and freedom.

2.4.2 Protection enhancement

The drive for the most extensive protection is a natural consequence of regarding intellectual resources as property. Then, renouncing time restrictions of protection is seemingly obvious because traditional property is not transferred (granted) for a limited period of time (which is the case with patents, for instance). There are obviously legal measures that may cause loss of property upon a lapse of time, for instance, usucaption. However, it is of exceptional nature and requires fairly stringent pre-conditions to be met. In other words: if an owner is in any way interested in an asset, then the time limit of usucaption may be easily interrupted. Thus, if intellectual property were to be property within its full meaning, it would be hard to find any reason for its time restriction. However, it is not difficult to become aware of a number of negative consequences arising from such an approach. It would above all mean negating the perennial foundation underlying the intellectual property law that constitutes the grounds for exclusive rights to be granted provided that unrestricted dissemination of the construct can be expected (relatively quickly).

Copyright underscores the aim for extension of legal protection of intellectual property, the time limit of which has been repeatedly increased in recent decades. It has been achieved in contravention of elementary logic pertaining to intellectual property law, founded on incentives to create, because such changes were also made to constructs *ex post*. In those cases the protection was strengthened although it did not have any impact upon the level of incentives to create those specific works. However, it was possible thanks to propertisation of intangible resources.

Furthermore, copyright has always substantially incorporated itself into time-unrestricted entitlements arising from ownership. An author's copyright (for instance, the right to place an author's name and surname on the work that the author has created) is not time-restricted contrary to an author's property rights, the current duration of which – as a rule – expires 70 years after the creator's death. However, there is some essential part of an author's copyright that still remains in contravention to the classic understanding of ownership, for it cannot be assigned to any third party (neither under an agreement nor as an inheritance). Ownership of tangible assets is not subject to such limitations.

Propertisation is connected to the adverse effects arising from the emphasising the free-rider problem within the framework of intangible resources management (Lemley, 2004, p. 1079). Free riders are dangerous for the system only when an intellectual property creator fails to cover the cost of its creation and generate a reasonable surplus. Empirical data, however, indicates that only a small number of free riders contribute to the development of such circumstances. Majority of them would merely renounce its purchase in case when an intangible asset is effectively protected. Thus, relaxing the protective measures will not directly influence a creator's revenue (we may only consider whether it indirectly diminishes the advantage of legitimate purchasers that, having paid a fee, degrade their competitiveness and have no comparative advantage over the free riders).

According to the report 'Circles of culture – social circulation of content' (Filiciak, Tarkowski, & Hofmokl, 2012), persons who often use unauthorised sources are at the same time the most active consumers of legitimate content. In other words – persons downloading movies or music from 'illegitimate' services in the Internet are the same persons who most often go to the cinema and concerts. Given such data, they are hard to be regarded as standard free riders. They ultimately account for the largest source of income earned by creators.

It is also hardly possible to estimate the losses incurred by the phonographic industry based on the formula: the number of unauthorised copies × price per copy. The teenagers, having saved 10,000 albums on their hard disc, cannot be expected to spend $100,000 on such a collection should unauthorised access be effectively denied. Thus, it is not so obvious that the free-rider problem influences creators' income because it is beyond any doubt that only a minor number of those albums would be bought anyway. Such a detriment to creators' income is not enough to place the free-rider problem at the centre of the architecture of the intellectual property management system. Naturally, it neither means that the issue should be utterly marginalised. Some limitations and restrictions are needed but they cannot be so extensive as to adversely impact positive effects arising from diffusion of intangible resources, which will be elaborated upon in the subchapter dedicated to directed diffusion.

The above considerations in no way suggest that no protection is required. However, hasty extrapolation of the tangible assets ownership framework (particularly the option of dogmatic treatment of ownership as a set of unrestricted rights) leaves no room for development of such a system that would facilitate creators to operate within effective business models and would concurrently not bring about excessive social losses. The aforementioned propertisation-oriented approach substantially contributes to the intensification of the Tragedy of Intangible Abundance, which is neither beneficial for creators nor for the society.

2.5 Intensified complexity of innovation

Contrary to the aforementioned causes of the Tragedy of Intangible Abundance, in this case, it is impossible to indicate the guilty parties. Deepening complexity of innovative projects is not reproachable. It neither is the outcome of deliberate strategies of any entities. However, it is one of the inherent and imminent effects of technological progress (Sweet & Eterovic, 2019). Nonetheless, that complexity is the source of many problems addressed in this book.

Each software incorporates numerous diverse ideas and large projects implement thousands of them. Google has estimated smartphones to incorporate even 250,000 of them. In 2004 GNU/Linux system was estimated to use approximately 100,000 patented constructs. According to D. Ravicher, the very core of Linux could have prospectively infringed 283 patents at that time (Stallman, 2011).

It bears noting that the studies (Wonglimpiyarat, 2005) do not confirm the intuitive thesis that increasing complexity of projects corresponds with extension of individual steps of the innovation process. Thus, it is groundless to take advantage of the argument of intensified complexity for the purpose of forcing the amplification or extension or of legal protection of inventions. The cited studies have not recognised the reason for that surprising state of affairs, namely the fact that a more complex project requires higher capital expenditures but in the contemporary economy such activities are undertaken by increasingly larger and stronger corporations that are capable of intensifying the efforts in a comparatively short time thanks to enormous resources at their disposal.

When considering complex innovative projects we must include global value chains, because even the largest companies need support at various stages of designing and manufacturing products. The contemporary institutional framework prefers larger players to a great extent, which raises some concerns. This is not due to lower organisational capacity of small- and medium-sized companies to search for partners in other parts of the world. They face the barrier due to insufficient opportunities to benefit from tax optimisation and a global intellectual property model that rewards a (patent) arms race.

That cold war metaphor is elaborated upon in the subsequent chapter. For the purpose of these considerations, we can state that small-sized companies are defenceless if they do not possess a large patent portfolio even when they undertake creative activity instead of imitating. They are not able to deter other players from bringing a case to court against them, for they are incapable of realistically threatening with a counter-claim. A small-sized company is bound to fail, given the high unpredictability of intellectual property-related litigation after having been strongly (broadly) attacked. Even if it wins, legal assistance costs may turn out to be too difficult to bear.

Therefore, there are two trends that account for the difficult position of smaller companies. On the one hand, it is natural – arising from the very essence of complexity – to favour large-sized companies. On the other hand, the institutional framework multiplies the adverse impacts instead of mitigating the threats resulting from the first mechanism. In consequence, smaller companies find it hard to achieve an advantageous position in global value chains.

Furthermore, even start-ups that are strongly determined to maintain independence and develop some interesting product often find themselves helpless. They can be blackmailed in a more or less sophisticated manner. They may either let a huge corporation buy them out or be destroyed. It is relatively easy to destroy for a large corporation even when using legitimate methods. Sometimes it is enough to communicate to the mass media that a company is working on a kindred construct (which effectively discourages majority of investors from funding the start-up). In other cases it is necessary to incorporate a similar functionality (similar to the one offered by the start-up) into some larger project implementable by a corporation. Even if it will be imperfect, it will still become an applicable standard because of the incomparably larger number of users.

Intensifying complexity of innovative projects is almost always connected to software issues. Often such constructs constitute some type of software (although hardware also happens to be equally important).

Thus, it is still another context in which the adverse impact of software patenting is so apparent, especially in the form based on functional claims (which has been addressed in section 2.1).

References

Alikhan, S., Mashelkar, R. A., & Martinez, C. (2006). *Valuation and Exploitation of Intellectual Property* (p. 217). Paris: OECD.

Allison, J. R., Lamley, M. A., & Schwartz, D. L. (2015). Our divided patent system, *82*(3), 1073–1154.

Bessen, J. (2011). A Generation of software patents. *Boston University School of Law Working Paper*, vol 18, 1–30.

Bessen, J., & Hunt, R. M. (2007). An empirical look at software patents. *Journal of Economics & Management Strategy, 16*(1), 157–189. http://doi.org/10.1111/j.1530-9134.2007.00136.x

Bessen, J., & Meurer, M. J. (2008). *Patent Failure* (pp. 1–347). Princeton, NJ and Oxford: Princeton University Press.

Biga, B. (2017). Ekonomiczna analiza odmienności własności intelektualnej i materialnej na przykładzie patentu. *Studia Ekonomiczne. Zeszyty Naukowe Uniwersytetu Ekonomicznego W Katowicach, 312,* 18–29.

Boldrin, M., & Levine, D. K. (2008). *Against Intellectual Monopoly* (pp. 1–309). Cambridge: Cambridge University Press.

Boldrin, M., & Levine, D. K. (2013). The case against patents. *The Journal of Economic Perspectives, 27*(1), 3–22. http://doi.org/10.1257/jep.27

Bounfour, A. (2003). *The Management of Intangibles: The Organisation's Most Valuable Assets* (pp. 1–337). London: Routledge.

Cambell-Kelly, M. (2005). Not all bad: An historical perspective on so ware patents. *Michigan Telecommunications and Technology Law Review, 11*(2), 192–248.

Elkin-Koren, N., & Salzberger, E. M. (2013). *The Law and Economics of Intellectual Property in the Digital Age* (pp. 1–305). New York: Routledge.

Fijałkowska, J. (2012). Analiza porównawcza wybranych metod pomiaru i wyceny kapitału intelektualnego. *Zarządzanie I Finanse, 1,* 415–425.

Filiciak, M., Tarkowski, A., & Hofmokl, J. (2012). Obiegi kultury. Społeczna cyrkulacja treści. Raport z badań.

Geodecki, T. (2008). Pomiar innowacyjności gospodarki przy użyciu pośrednich i bezpośrednich wskaźników innowacji. *Zarządzanie Publiczne, 3*(5), 27–50.

Graham, S., & Vishnubhakat, S. (2013). Of smart phone wars and software patents. *The Journal of Economic Perspectives, 27*(1), 67–85. http://doi.org/10.1257/jep.27.L67

Hunter, L. C., Webster, E., & Wyatt, A. (2005). Measuring Intangible Investment. Intellectual Property Research Institute of Australia, Working Paper No. 18/05

Lallement, R. (2017). *Intellectual Property and Innovation Protection.* Hoboken, NJ: John Wiley & Sons. http://doi.org/10.1002/9781119473800

Lea, D. (2008). The expansion and restructuring of intellectual property and its implications for the developing world. *Ethical Theory and Moral Practice, 11*(1), 37–60.

Lemley, M. A. (2004). Property, intellectual property, and free riding. *Texas Law Review, 83*, 1031–1087.

Lemley, M. A. (2012, October 12). Software patents and the return of functional claiming. *Wisconsin Law Review.* http://doi.org/10.2139/ssrn.2117302

Lemley, M. A., & Shapiro, C. (2005). Probabilistic patents. *The Journal of Economic Perspectives, 19*(2), 75–98.

Li, Y. (2019). The current dilemma and future of software patenting. *IIC-International Review of Intellectual Property and Competition Law, 50*(7), 823–859.

Mann, R. J. (2005). Do patents facilitate financing in the software industry? *Texas Law Review, 83*, 961–1030.

Miller, S. P. (2014). "Fuzzy" software patent boundaries and high claim construction reversal Rates. *Stanford Technology Law Review, 17*, 809–841.

Oleksak, M. M., & Adams, M. (2010). *Intangible Capital* (pp. 1–192). Santa Barbara, CA: Praeger.

Rifkin, J. (2014). *The Zero Marginal Cost Society.* New York: St. Martin's Press.

Sebastian, S., Dumitrascu, D., & Pele, A. (2017). Recognizing and valuating intangible resources-Major difficulties in organisational management. *Management of Sustainable Development, 9*(1), 35.

Shapiro, C. (2001). Navigating the patent thicket: Cross licenses, patent pools, and standard-setting. *Wisconsin Law Review,* 1–35. http://doi.org/10.2139/ssrn.273550

Sichelman, T. (2010). Commercializing patents. *Stanford Law Review, 62*(2), 341–414.

Skrzypek, E. (2014). Pomiar kapitału intelektualnego w przedsiębiorstwie – aspekty metodyczne. *Studia Metodologiczne, 32*, 95–116.

Stallman, R. (2011, August). Beware: Europe's 'unitary patent' could mean unlimited software patents. *The Guardian.*

Stiglitz, J. E. (2008). Economic foundations of intellectual property rights. *Duke Law Journal, 57*(6), 1693–1724.

Sweet, C., & Eterovic, D. (2019). Do patent rights matter? 40 years of innovation, complexity and productivity. *World Development, 115*, 78–93.

Wasilewska, M. (2015). *Wycena i raportowanie kapitału intelektualnego w spółkach giełdowych.* Wrocław.

Wonglimpiyarat, J. (2005). Does complexity affect the speed of innovation? *Technovation, 25*(8), 865–882. http://doi.org/10.1016/j.technovation.2004.01.010

3 Indications of Tragedy of Intangible Abundance

3.1 Intellectual property demand and supply mismatch

The intellectual property demand and supply mismatch is the major indication of the Tragedy of Intangible Abundance (Schwartz, 2016). It needs to be explicitly underlined that intangible resources are not goods that may be referred to in terms of the statement: 'the more of them, the better'. A number of simplified analyses completely disregard:

1 The costs of innovation acceleration
2 Adequately matching supply and demand

3.1.1 The cost of innovation acceleration

Innovation has become the Holy Grail for business and science. Moreover, tax incentives are usually awarded regardless of the real outcomes of innovation-oriented activities focusing primarily on the eligibility of costs, and on purely declarative reporting. High risk is obviously inherent in innovation-oriented activities, and the support systems need to show notable tolerance of failed projects (because the majority of them will fail), but rarely is the basic economic analysis of costs and benefits conducted. It may be somewhat justified since a high risk of failure is inherent in truly innovative activities. Therefore, it could be rational for a part of the risk of eventual failure to be shared by the state. Since it is a considerable cost that is hard to bear for private companies, especially smaller ones, while the pursuit of innovation is a shared goal for both the government and business.

The problem is that those circumstances do not entitle anyone to disregard the issue of efficiency. Risk management fundamentals or operational efficiency assessments are too rarely taken into account for the purpose of awarding financial assistance. On the part of entrepreneurs themselves, there are no appropriate stimuli as they regard public innovation-targeted financial assistance as an easy, non-binding form of raising funds.

3.1.2 Adequately matching supply and demand

It is neither assessed whether innovation-oriented activities are tailored to demand. Naturally, it must be stated that such an undertaking would encounter massive limitations since in the case of novel constructs it is impossible to identify specific needs a priori and even harder to assess the related readiness to pay for them. That, however, does not mean that demand assessment is not feasible at all.

In such a case one cannot expect market mechanisms to automatically direct activities aiming at creation of intangible assets to meet the greatest demand. The pharmaceutical industry may be a very vivid example as it focuses on the marketing of unsophisticated painkillers and anti-inflammatory drugs (creating intellectual property mainly in the form of widely recognisable trademarks). On the other hand, novel medication research seems to be relatively underfunded – especially for rare diseases. Such research is subject to substantial risk, and the potential market is much smaller but with notable demand, usually inelastic in nature.

That, however, does not mean that – generally speaking – the demand for effective medication is met by subsequent releases of paracetamol- or ibuprofen-derived tablets, notwithstanding the superficial analysis that would prove steady growth of the total value of intangible resources due to the growing strength of trademarks. The state government policy aiming at prevention of such problems is discussed in the following chapter, on the grounds of the American Orphan Drug Act.

Thus, there is a huge supply of intellectual property in the pharmaceutical industry (mainly trademarks) but many needs and requirements (demand for novel medication) remain unsatisfied. Thus, the estimated increase in intangible resources in the economy/industry/company does not mean in itself any higher efficiency or better problem-solving or satisfying consumers' needs and requirements. And that is despite that the primary function of intangible resources is to enhance the value of tangible resources in use. That is, however, feasible provided that intangible resources supply and demand have been matched.

That problem is vivid when the increasingly growing percentage share of intangible resources in companies' value is compared to the percentage share of intangible resources in the added value of products sold. Such estimates may obviously be inaccurate due to the intangible resources valuation methods that are far from satisfactory as well as too simple or even primitive methodology applied by the WIPO. Juxtapositions of even such data, however, prove the striking discordance (the related charts have been displayed in Chapter 1). More and more valuable (or better visible) intangible resources do not seem to equal the higher percentage share in the added value of products sold. Furthermore, it is plausible to state that intangible assets account for a growing percentage share in companies' value in spite of the fact that their percentage share in companies' assets does not grow, which means that their efficiency is decreasing. Ergo: either intangible resources management problems accumulate or they are simultaneously increasingly common and less and less valuable.

3.2 Intellectual property law has become an arms-race field

The current intellectual property management practices make it hard to avoid the metaphor of the arms race and the Cold War, because companies patent in order to deter opponents and mitigate the risk of being sued (attacked) instead of building obstacles that will prevent immediate competitors. The arsenal that is being built does not serve the company itself nor is to be used for hostile actions. It is rather to serve as protection against being sued. Competitors will be less inclined to sue the higher the risk of a counterclaim is.

The Cold War metaphor is also adequate for other reasons. Similarly to the arms race between the United States and the USSR, dummy munitions constituted a considerable part of the arsenal, just like in the area of intellectual property where a huge number of patents do not constitute any combat strength, i.e. they do not reflect any strictly business-related strength. Their usefulness may be considered exclusively in the context of deterrence. Sticking to the Cold War metaphor, it cannot remain unnoticed that, if it comes to any actual 'detonation' (although it happens relatively rarely – as little as 1.5% is estimated to be the object of litigation), the effects of such a detonation may be enormous, even 'nuclear' – even if it assures a successful court resolution, it will undoubtedly also cause considerable collateral damage. The studies conducted by PWC (Barry, Arad, Ansell, Cartier, & Lee, 2016, 2016) indicate that the average awarded damages for infringement of intellectual property range from USD 3.8 to 9.2 million in the United States.

M. Boldrin and D. Levine (2013, p. 9) are among those who draw attention to the absurdity of contemporary usage of intellectual property. The contemporary game comes down to balancing the patent portfolios owned by major players, which has nothing in common with the promotion of innovativeness. The effect being that, in the area of balanced patent portfolios, no company can bring a case to court against another. Thus, it is the same state of affairs as if there were no legal protections in the form of monopolies. That, however, brings about a new but considerable category of expenses – entry barriers for new companies that, in order to participate in the game, do not only have to create an innovative construct but also develop a much larger security 'enclosure' and create a relevant patent portfolio. In this sense, patent law not only fails to support innovation but is actually a sphere of activity that hampers it.

3.2.1 Peacock's tail effect

The book 'Darwin Economy' by R. Frank argues that economic mechanisms are better described by evolutionary economics (Nelson, Dosi, & Helfat, 2018) rather than those described by A. Smith. That, most of all, means the risk of falling into the 'peacock's tail' trap. Evolutionary mechanisms made it more 'beneficial' to have a bigger tail, because reproductive success was dependent on it to a great extent. Male peacocks that had the (relatively) most impressive tail were most attractive. In consequence, tails of next generations evolved to be more and more impressive. Advantage, however, is always relative, thus within subsequent repetition of procreative competitions, success was achieved by male peacocks that had increasingly bigger tails – since that was the only way to (relatively) increase their chances.

That process, elementary from the point of view of evolution, made peacocks a very easy target for predators. Not only were they easily noticeable but had limited defensive capabilities. All that was explainable in individual cases within the context of relative advantage actually lead to fatal consequences for the species as a whole.

A similar phenomenon may be noted in the case of accumulating intangible resources by enterprises, for which a major motivation is the fear of lagging behind in terms of accumulated intangible resources. Moreover, that fear is somewhat justified – a company may be an easy target of any attack if it lacks an adequately large patent portfolio – thus being deprived of any chance for an effective countersuit. As such it becomes a comparatively easy, actually a defenceless, target.

One needs to bear in mind that this mechanism is not based on development of a large-sized patent portfolio in absolute terms. Its usefulness will always depend on comparison with the competitors' portfolio size. And since the majority of companies aim at enhancing their portfolios, it is necessary to possess a growing number of patents in order to achieve a relatively safe position. In consequence, similarly to peacocks, pursuing a comparative advantage exposes the whole species – the economy – to the risk of becoming more and more dysfunctional.

A strong stimulus is required to challenge the peacock's tail trap. In theoretical terms, it may be extensive, bottom-up coordinated activities aiming at goals similar to those regarding the global reduction of nuclear arsenals. On the other hand, that analogy also reveals the problems with such initiatives. Possible law amendments that could curb the benefits of thoughtless extension of patent portfolios are elaborated upon in the subsequent chapter.

3.3 Patent thickets and entry barriers

Patent flooding is the obvious consequence of non-restrictive procedures of assessing patent application forms by Patent Offices (according to the World Intellectual Property Organisation, over a million of patents are granted on an annual basis). It needs to be underlined that although the very implications of the intellectual property law result in entry barriers (exclusive rights are to contribute to competitive advantage), the contemporary practices go beyond the model-based framework. Notwithstanding the non-restrictive requirement of non-obviousness that is the major cause of the aforementioned patent flooding, today's entry barriers took on the nature of patent thickets.

Abundance of patents and the immense ambiguity of patent boundaries cause a considerable risk of entering a market and the created barriers to entry are much more solid than the sum of boundaries created by respective patents. That means that the difficulty does not only arise from the fact that some area is already effectively protected. The problem is that it is hard to pave a safe (even when taking into consideration a certain error rate) path for own – creative and fair – business operations.

Some of the authors (Gątkowski, Dietl, Skrok, Whalen, & Rockett, 2018), however, highlight the positive effects of patent thickets, perceived as an opportunity to raise a patent bonus high enough (since that bonus – according to the cited author – does not cover the cost of an ordinary patent). It is, however, a peculiarity since the attempt to correct the dysfunction of the intellectual property law is founded on one of its reasons. That is a vicious circle. A patent must admittedly be beneficial, which should generate some surplus in excess of the costs incurred. That is viable only when an average quality (value) of a patent is adequately high (then the removal of the worst ones will allow for covering of incurred costs), and the cases brought to court will become more predictable (which is hindered by the existing patent thickets). Thus, patent thickets may hardly be any remedy for a relatively low patent bonus (apart from the pharmaceutical industry).

The cited authors (Gątkowski et al., 2018) also draw attention to the fact that

> reduced entry into patenting in new technology areas may also be welfare-reducing, for at least two reasons. First, there is the obvious argument that the benefits from more innovation may exceed any business stealing costs (...), so that some desirable innovation may be deterred by high entry costs. Even if this were not true, there is no reason to believe that firms that do not enter into patenting due to thickets are those we wish to deter. Given the incumbency advantage, it is likely that the failure to enter into patenting in these areas reflects less innovation by those who bring the most original ideas, that is, by those who are inventing 'outside the box'.

Taking advantage of patents for the purpose of creating entry barriers to prevent competitors from entering the market is not an aberration in itself (Harhoff, Graevenitz, & Wagner, 2016). It is the essence of the immanent goal of patenting. The created entry barrier is the bonus for innovativeness and disclosure of one's invention to society. The pathology that is one of the indications of the Tragedy of Intangible Abundance arises from the 'game' that is played by the top market players and as such contributes to much higher barriers than those derived from the mere impossibility to use a specific innovative construct that has been patented.

The term 'specific' needs to be highlighted. However, given the low quality of patents with boundaries that are ambiguous, competitors are forced to curb business operations and include a safety margin, which causes the zone of exclusiveness to be strikingly disproportionate to the scale of a patented invention. That effect may additionally be intensified by the fear aroused from an innovative debutante, who, lacking an impressive patent portfolio is unable to threaten with a countersuit. That is still another consequence of the aforementioned intellectual arms race that, in the context of the top market players, transforms into some form of Cold War. However, in the case of smaller companies, the patent arsenal may be used for hampering a new player from entering the already divided market.

Such actions are effective but are in contravention of the basic implications that have underlain the creation of legal protection of inventions. In the model-based framework, the entry barrier is the reward proportional to the disclosed novel construct. Within the caricaturized framework described here, patents become the barrier instead of being the shield for independent innovators. Therefore, they are often used for the purpose of negotiations that take the form of blackmailing when a large corporation tables an irrefusable offer to a start-up to be taken over. Without a wide protective patent umbrella, a small company may be blocked from developing its product.

3.3.1 Patent pools

Patent thickets are related with the growing popularity of patent pools. Those are agreements made by a couple of enterprises regarding safe and joint use of intellectual property. Each of the enterprises entering into such an agreement agrees for unlimited free-of-charge use of its resources by all the other agreement parties. In return, it is obviously entitled to do the same. Patent pools thus constitute cooperation based on automatic cross-licensing. It may also be the so called blanket licensing allowing for subsequent resources to be used based on pre-agreed principles.

On the one hand, patent pools may be perceived as an indication of modern cooperation within an industry. From the perspective of the Tragedy of Intangible Abundance, one needs to notice entry barriers that are created by such activities. The intellectual property law applied in that way creates limitations that will be much harder to combat for new market entrants, especially smaller companies, than would be the sum of challenges resulting from individual patents. Within this meaning it is an aberration – as the intellectual property law has not aimed at taking care of smaller companies in order to protect them from threats on the part of larger market players. Patent pooling arrangements are obviously flexible, which provides for companies possessing weaker patent portfolios to enter into the agreement. Then they are obligated to make specific payments to balance the potential disproportions (Boldrin & Levine, 2008, p. 63).

There are many great examples, where companies voluntarily contribute to the patent pool to make a given technology even better and eventually more popular. The Bluetooth patent pool is a good example, where competitors have expanded the market for their individual products and services.

The Author has conducted research in the Technology Park Kraków (http://www.kpt.krakow.pl/en/). It has revealed the popularity of the approach based on such a rule: if I sell, for example, intelligent lighting system, I am deeply interested in the popularisation of Bluetooth standard – even in favour of my direct competitors and companies from diverse branches. My biggest barrier is the size of the market – which means the number of Bluetooth device users. Therefore, the more popular and the better Bluetooth is, the greater opportunities I have got. Therefore, I want to contribute to this standard (Biga, Unpublished).

However, sometimes patent pools account for a sophisticated way to build extremely strong entry barriers for competitors. We have examples (Ehrnsperger & Tietze, 2019) that such bundles of patents are designed to create patent thickets. Then we do not talk about open standard but we can use a metaphor of the minefield. This is a very harmful situation because it blocks innovation and dishonestly destroys competition. Patent thickets create legal monopolies much stronger than the institution of patent was originally designed for.

Popularity of patent pooling proves patents to be less and less perceived as the source of a company's competitive advantage but they simply constitute one of the tools used for creating entry barriers. Within this context it is hard to acknowledge that the time-restricted monopoly replaceable with acceleration of research and public disclosure is still effective in terms of the principles underlying intellectual property law.

3.4 'Patent trolls' (non-practising-entities)

'Patent trolls' are most often related with software patenting. 'Patent trolls' take advantage of imperfections of the industrial property law and in that way they often earn high profits. They most often take over constructs that have already been publicised and have not been patented, although they do not intend to incorporate them into their products or they buy patents from bankrupt companies at heavily discounted rates. They subsequently threaten companies – advanced products of which allegedly infringe their patents – that they may be faced with expensive litigation, usually aiming to achieve voluntary out of court settlements. 'Patent trolls' are so effective in creating proposals for settlements that it is often accepted even in the situation when lawyers employed by blackmailed companies see little chance for success of such litigation.

The discussed category of entities is highly heterogeneous. It includes both 'trolls' that claim compensation in the amount equivalent to a few hundred thousand dollars based on minor construct nuances, and those bringing cases to courts against global giants to claim compensation amounting to hundreds of millions of Dollars (Bessen & Meurer, 2013). The colloquial definition of a 'troll' could also include universities and other research centres that often come into possession of patents notwithstanding their lack of desire to use them for commercial purposes. That is, however, an exceptional example, the peculiarity of which arises from cardinal differences in the motivation of those entities. For that reason, they cannot designated as 'patent trolls'.

The term 'patent troll' is not acceptable for some of the researchers ((Weber, 2016) who regard it as too pejorative. Instead do they suggest the non-practising entity (NPE) emphasising the part of its definition that corresponds to the lack of independent commercialisation of inventions. The pejorative term 'troll' results from the stress put on the peculiar strategy that those entities implement. It is characteristic of extreme opportunism and considerable legal aggression toward those alleged to have caused infringement.

One needs to certainly be restrained in labelling entities with the term 'patent trolls'. Hasty defining would make Thomas Edison their king, who is considered to be the role model of an inventor to follow as far as social awareness is concerned. For decades he was accountable for the largest number of patents in terms of individual inventors as he had received 1093 of them, although initially very few of them were incorporated into specific products. But, he built his fortune also on patents that were practically not used in practice, and some inventions were patented by him only in order to hinder innovations. Those circumstances account for considering him to be a 'troll' (McDonough, 2006, p. 198).

Antagonists (Cohen, Gurun, & Kominers, 2019) of NPEs focus on several fundamental issues. They primarily point to the low quality of patents obtained by those entities, which results in material and factual infringement rarely occurring, and concurrently affects the quality of the whole system of invention legal protection. Widespread nature of achieved settlements results rather from risk aversion and fear of litigation costs to be incurred by those who happen to be sued. 'Trolls' also curb innovativeness of companies striving to commercialise inventions. Those companies do not usually copy constructs found in troll portfolios but achieve the same deliverables within independently conducted research.

Impotence of state governments in combating 'patent trolls' has forced a group of huge IT corporations (e.g. Google, Sony, Cisco,

Philips, IBM, Hewlett-Packard) to set up the Allied Security Trust, intended to buy patent rights that could possibly be targeted by 'trolls'. However, not only global giants happen to become victims of the NPE. The fact that the Allied Security Trust was set up mainly by IT companies results from the overwhelming convictions that the majority of patents claimed by the NPE centres on software.

The subject literature (Choi & Gerlach, 2018; Xiaodong, 2017) also includes numerous examples in support of the NPE. It indicates the fact that they create an extremely useful secondary patent market. It allows, inter alia, to recover financial liquidity for companies undergoing financial troubles as well as to facilitate new companies to come into possession of basic intellectual property resources. However, one needs to bear in mind that such a market does not support innovativeness.

It is also underlined that the existence of NPEs reinforces the position of small enterprises that often face intellectual property infringement from large enterprises. Due to disproportions in budgeted legal assistance expenses, they have sizeable difficulties in opposing such incursions. Furthermore, 'patent trolls' often become those minor enterprises, which have been pushed out from the market and that have been deprived of the opportunity to sell their products and services and now, by initiating patent-based litigation, they see the chance for at least partial compensation of costs incurred in the creation of an invention. Authors defending NPEs draw attention also to the fact that thanks to such entities it is possible to take advantage of more effective methods of real protection of individual investors by means of substance-based, law-based experience sharing.

J. F. McDonough (2006, pp. 227–228) calls NPEs 'patent dealers' and interprets their role through the prism of the market they create, and which should be governed by the same principles that govern markets for conventional goods. He claims that the liquidity delivered by 'trolls' contributes to efficiency and facilitates valuation of patents, thus NPEs prove to be a natural and positive phenomenon from the point of view of economic principles. He writes that they are rather gentle giants instead of spooky 'trolls', and according to some of the authors (Risch, 2012, p. 458), their operations are assessed on the grounds of a half-truth and myths that have accumulated around them. According to him, criticism is too often based on referring to isolated absurd patents and too hasty extrapolation of related comments onto the entirety of NPEs' operations.

It cannot be, however, denied that the majority of benefits seen by NPE supporters are indirect and the cause-effect relationship is not always clear. Moreover, the benefits attributed to NPE operations could be achieved – equally or even to a greater extent – by means of other, direct measures. Furthermore, when considering the balance of economic and social effects of 'troll' activity, the greatest importance is assigned to various costs – direct and indirect'.

Operations of 'patent trolls' hardly provide any net benefits for society. Calculations also indicate that costs generated by NPEs, that small- and medium-sized companies incur, are higher than the expenditures that 'trolls' are able to transfer onto innovations. Their operations also undoubtedly hinder the operations of innovative enterprises – increasing costs of numerous services and products – and discourage many entities from commencing business operations. In extreme cases they may even successfully block development of some promising construct. Their operations, however, most often resemble extortion.

Given the above, the need to regard the maximum limitation of patent trolls' operations is obvious, as one of the major objectives of reforming invention protection law. It is, however, impossible to have such practices discontinued completely without the abolition of patents. Even a system that will be better than the current one will not be resistant to the use of patents for purposes contravening the aim of this legal institution.

It is, however, necessary to note positive effects of changes in the case-law of American courts [RPX 2019]. It is currently harder for NPEs to expect a positive outcome (or even defer a sued project effectively) in the situation when a plaintiff does not use the object of the litigation for economic purposes. The total ban on NPEs' right to litigation would not be a good practice in the context of the democratic rule of law (Diessel, 2007, p. 305).

3.5 Ineffective legal intellectual property protection

It is indicated (Lemley & Shapiro, 2005, p. 77) that effectiveness of today's legal system of intellectual property protection means that legal monopolies do not provide for exclusion of others but rather for an exclusion attempt. This perspective is confirmed by research projects, including those cited by (Sampat, 2018, p. 5). The qualitative analysis of companies with a substantial R&D component proves a patent promise to be an insufficient stimulus to undertake innovation-oriented operations. The first analysis of that kind included 69 companies being in possession of 45,500 patents, and was conducted as early as in 1959. It was subsequently repeated. The companies were proven to earn R&D revenue from other sources in the majority of business areas. They most often rely on time advantage and pre-emptive rights, and those are the much stronger stimuli influencing business decision-making than unpredictable patent-based protection.

Furthermore, the studies carried out at the University of Cambridge (Taylor, Silberston, & Silberston, 1973), in which British companies were asked by how much would they reduce R&D expenses if patents were replaced with statutory licensing with associated modest royalties (which obviously means total abolition of the classical patenting under which a monopoly allows to fix a price at a very high level). The average R&D expense reduction was indicated at 8%. The exception was the pharmaceutical industry in which abolition of patenting would cause the reduction by as much as 64%.

3.5.1 Denial of reasons for emergence of legal monopolies

The analysis of the actual use of the intellectual property law makes it impossible to defend the current practices based on the model aims that guided the introduction of legal protection for intellectual property and that were regarded as axioms in consecutive ages of development of that domain of law. The Venetian Act of 1474 was the first act of law to govern industrial property. Until the second half of the twentieth century its implications had not been challenged at all and a substantial part of contemporary researchers claim that the system derived from its foundations will sufficiently protect invention. Its opening provisions indicate the purpose that the invention protection system is to serve:

> There are in this city, and also there come temporarily by reason of its greatness and goodness, men from different places and most clever minds, capable of devising and inventing all manner of ingenious contrivances. And should it be provided that the works and contrivances invented by them, others having seen them could not make them and take their honour, men of such kind would exert their minds, invent and make things which would be of no small utility and benefit to our State.

The will to ensure an adequate supply of valuable intellectual property is the reason why society agrees to accept the inconveniences of time-restricted monopolies (based on patents or copyright). However, the protection of patent rights, which has effectively been serving that purpose for hundreds of years, is no longer tailored to the contemporary economic reality (Indradewi, 2020).

In most general terms, the most effective legal invention protection system is the one that, on the one hand, will sufficiently encourage to research and share inventions, and on the other hand, will mitigate the adverse impact of monopolies that may emerge in that context. The optimal solution is a state of affairs that will assure the lowest possible social costs while investors are encouraged to create. Such a model perspective is complicated due to the fact that the state of inventors (their form of existence) is not binary in nature: inventing/not inventing. There is a whole spectrum of intermediary states in which inventors undertake activity to a varied extent. Making the clause 'sufficiently encouraged to create' more precise would not be easy, either.

It may be assumed that the more inventors benefit – and the more cost the society incurs – are assured by law, the more intensively they work and the more capital expenditures are spent on research and in consequence more inventions emerge. From the societal perspective, however, the fact of creating a large number of inventions is not of value in itself because, if their accessibility is strictly limited, it will only be beneficial to a minor group of people while irritating the majority. That issue may well be depicted by the search for a cancer cure: it would undoubtedly be socially more reasoned to create such a legal regime in which it would be invented five years later but would be affordable to 50% of the sick population than to invent it earlier but for the first 20 years only 0.5% of the richest sick population could afford it. The pursuit of accelerating research and encouraging inventors to create as fast as possible is not an absolute goal. It is necessary to balance to what extent will accessibility – namely social benefits – be limited due to legal regulations beneficial to inventors.

Furthermore, the Tragedy of Intangible Abundance shows that the considerations cannot be limited to the above framework because today's reality of legal invention protection does not only bring about 'common' inconveniences related to a time-restricted patent-based monopoly. On the one hand, they cause a number of other drawbacks that have been mentioned previously. On the other hand, the very core – essence of patenting – is less and less effective. Ergo: new circumstances have emerged that are a social cost, alongside simultaneous marginalisation of the benefits, that was to be the provision of stimuli to create and disclose innovations.

The studies (Sampat, 2018, p. 20) show that the classical justification for patent-based protection works in some sectors of the economy. In the majority of cases, however, patents are not a sufficient incentive. They do indeed happen to be used for other strategic purposes (but those that are apparently in contravention of the original idea of intellectual property protection). The substantial volume of innovations have been created and still are created beyond the patenting system. Reinforcement of patent-based protection brings about a slightly higher patenting inclination but that is not necessarily correlated with larger innovations. Stronger patent-based protection will not arouse more interest in researching tropical diseases. Patents have little influence on even highly valuable investments in social terms, the market for which is, however, not big enough (with an adequate purchasing power). They are, therefore, not able to substitute for such mechanisms as the publicly funded system of research or awards (Sampat, 2018, p. 20).

3.5.2 Unpredictability of court cases

Differences among sectors of the economy seem to be crucial in the area under consideration (OECD, 2006). Effectiveness of legal intellectual property protection measures in a variety of business areas may be proven most of all by judicial statistics, including first of all the percentage of cases in which a patent holder turned out to be the winner. In the case of pharmaceutical patents, such a percentage accounts for 57.8%, mechanical patents – 54%, software patents – 40.2%, and biotechnological patents – as little as 32%. One may arrive at the conclusion that a patent tailors its quality to the industry (Allison, Lamley, & Schwartz, 2015). Moreover, a lost court case does not only fail to provide for compensation but in many cases it may bring about patent annulment, which will cause a patent holder to be deprived of benefits and the chance to counteract possible subsequent infringements.

That shows how weak are today's patents. Patent Offices award monopolies for constructs that are difficult to defend in the contradictory procedure (which leads to greater scrutiny). As a rule, in the patent application procedure there is no party involved that would be in opposition to the patent applicant. The existing right to file objections is not any sufficient barrier. In consequence, we see a low selectivity of patent applications. As it has already been mentioned, Patent Offices do not interpret patentability even in a moderately restrictive manner.

In the Polish intellectual property case-law, the plaintiff's success coefficient approximates to 40% (Biga, Możdżeń, Unpublished). That figure includes the case-law awarding the claim fully or partially (both of them are reported jointly). That confirms the figures reported in the United States. In Poland, i.e., a country having a totally different tradition of law and economic development, legal protection is also very difficult to be enforced in a court of law.

Moreover, my research proves such large differences in the case-law represented by respective courts. Analysing the data, considerable differences in court procedures are noticeable and arise from specific practices in respective courts. However, those differences cannot be justified, given the binding legal regulations. The court procedure obviously influences both costs and time as well as substance-based grounds and reasons of court decisions. Therefore, those are additional factors accounting for high unpredictability of enforcement of intellectual property rights before courts.

The above-mentioned uncertainties translate into decisions made by prospective inventors. Since in its classical understanding, the exclusive right promise is to stimulate innovation, the conviction of high unpredictability of effective enforcement will adversely impact the created incentives. Moreover, it is accompanied by increasing social costs of legal invention protection since the weaker protection observed by creators will not automatically mean better accessibility of inventions. Potential competitors cannot regard inventions protected even by very weak patents as equivalent to the unpatented ones. Inconveniences arising from a possible litigation mean that, even if it has no chance of success, such litigation entails the need to employ considerable resources and a comparatively long period of uncertainty.

Unpredictability of court cases cannot be regarded as an acceptable way of easing restrictiveness of protection regime since that way of easing is extremely ineffective. The emerging state of uncertainty and other inconveniences related with a court case constitute the source of costs from all perspectives: an innovator, competitor, or society.

References

Allison, J. R., Lamley, M. A., & Schwartz, D. L. (2015). Our divided patent system. *University of Chicago Law Review, 82*(3), 1073–1154.

Barry, C., Arad, R., Ansell, L., Cartier, M., & Lee, H. (2016). *2016 Patent Litigation Study: Are We at an Inflection Point?* New York: PricewaterhouseCoopers.

Bessen, J., & Meurer, M. J. (2013). The direct costs from NPE disputes. *Cornell Law Review, 99*, 387.

Boldrin, M., & Levine, D. K. (2008). *Against Intellectual Monopoly* (pp. 1–309). Cambridge: Cambridge University Press.

Boldrin, M., & Levine, D. K. (2013). The case against patents. *The Journal of Economic Perspectives, 27*(1), 3–22. http://doi.org/10.1257/jep.27

Choi, J. P., & Gerlach, H. (2018). A model of patent trolls. *International Economic Review, 59*(4), 2075–2106.

Cohen, L., Gurun, U. G., & Kominers, S. D. (2019). Patent trolls: Evidence from targeted firms. *Management Science, 65*(12), 5461–5486.

Diessel, B. H. (2007). Trolling for trolls: The pitfalls of the emerging market competition requirement for permanent injunctions in patent cases post-eBay. *Michigan Law Review, 106*, 305.

Ehrnsperger, J. F., & Tietze, F. (2019). Patent pledges, open IP, or patent pools? Developing taxonomies in the thicket of terminologies. *PloS One, 14*(8), e0221411.

Gątkowski, M., Dietl, M., Skrok, L., Whalen, R., & Rockett, K. (2018). Patent Thickets Identification. http://repository.essex.ac.uk/22928/1/ Towards%20a%20New%20Method%20for%20Patent%20Thickets%20 Identification_Oct_18_RP.pdf

Harhoff, D., Graevenitz, von, G., & Wagner, S. (2016). Conflict resolution, public goods, and patent thickets. *Management Science, 62*(3), 704–721.

Indradewi, A. A. S. N. (2020). Protection of intellectual property rights in international trade. *International Journal of Social Sciences, 3*(1), 13–16.

Lemley, M. A., & Shapiro, C. (2005). Probabilistic patents. *The Journal of Economic Perspectives, 19*(2), 75–98.

McDonough, J. F., III. (2006). The myth of the patent troll: An alternative view of the function of patent dealers in an idea economy. *Emory Law Journal, 56*, 189.

Nelson, R. R., Dosi, G., & Helfat, C. E. (2018). *Modern Evolutionary Economics: An Overview.* Cambridge: Cambridge University Press.

OECD. (2006). Creating value from intellectual assets, Paper presented at Meeting of OECD Council at Ministerial Level, Paris, 1–34.

Risch, M. (2012). Patent troll myths. *Seton Hall Law Review, 42*, 457–499.

Sampat, B. N. (2018). *A Survey of Empirical Evidence on Patents and Innovation* (No. w25383). National Bureau of Economic Research.

Schwartz, H. M. (2016). Wealth and secular stagnation: The role of industrial organization and intellectual property rights. *RSF: The Russell Sage Foundation Journal of the Social Sciences, 2*(6), 226–249.

Taylor, C. T., Silberston, A., & Silberston, Z. A. (1973). *The Economic Impact of the Patent System: A Study of the British Experience* (Vol. 23). Cambridge: Cambridge University Press.

Weber, L. (2016). *The Rise and Fall of the Patent Trolls: How They Lost the Public Relations Battle.* A Senior Project presented to The Faculty of the Journalism Department California Polytechnic State University, San

Luis Obispo. https://digitalcommons.calpoly.edu/cgi/viewcontent.cgi?
referer=https://scholar.google.pl/scholar?hl=pl&as_sdt=0%2C5&q=Web
er%2C++L.+%282016%29.+The+Rise+and+Fall+of+the+Patent+Trolls
%3A+How+They+Lost+the+Public+Relations+Battle.&btnG=&httpsre
dir=1&article=1108&context=joursp

Xiaodong, C. (2017). On patent trolls, non-practiced patents and actual use of
patents. *China Invention & Patent*, vol.83.

4 Toward openness – counteracting the Tragedy of Intangible Abundance

4.1 Systemic measures

The aim of this book is not only to describe reasons and manifestations of the Tragedy of Intangible Abundance but also to outline preventive measures. However, that is not easy. Complexity of the reasons underlying the current state of affairs makes it difficult to speak about totally successful mitigation of the related adverse impact. At best, one may strive to curb it. That is what the title Economics of Intellectual Property and Openness does. It is clear that a variety of actions are needed to be undertaken by diverse actors since – as the chapter about the causes of the Tragedy of Intangible Abundance defines it – the activities of numerous groups of entities have contributed to the emergence of the current problems. However, it is common to pursue greater (but not total) openness in intellectual property management that is to manifest itself in widespread conditional dissemination.

The postulated changes require, however, acceptance of several fundamental assumptions:

1 Intellectual property management requires tools that will be considerably different from the tools for tangible assets management.
2 Exclusive rights are rarely the best (nor should they be the default) form of intellectual property protection.
3 Within the contemporary economy (digital economy, in particular), business models that come forward with substantial amount of revenue to be earned from sources other than the core business often prove to be more effective.
4 Quality of patents and other exclusive rights should be verified in the course of the legal protection application procedure, and only in exceptional cases on the *ex-post* basis (for instance, before a court).

5   There are many other incentives to create intellectual property than a mere promise of a time-restricted monopoly (these incentives are at least as strong as legal ones).

These circumstances directly result from the considerations undertaken within the previous chapters. Specific applications are elaborated upon further in this chapter.

4.1.1 Amendments to the law

Within the context of intellectual property protection, postulates *de lege ferenda* are especially challenged. That is an extensively unified domain – governed by a number of international agreements. Furthermore, the binding regulations were shaped as early as in the nineteenth century. Thus, they are well-established. In order to amend them, a compromise among the state governments representing extremely contradictory interests would be necessary.

History, however, has shown that even comparatively minor amendments, such as redefining the extent of compulsory licensing or computer software protection, have caused considerable difficulties. Considerable tension has traditionally been visible between rich countries (representing mainly the northern hemisphere) and poor countries (mainly from the southern hemisphere). The former ones usually opt for very restrictive intellectual property protection. That is not surprising since they represent interests of technologically advanced companies and original medication producers, and their economies are knowledge-based economies to a great extent.

Developing countries are aware that they are not capable of competing effectively in global terms, given the restrictive intellectual property law. The majority of contemporary economic powers only pretended to protect intellectual property at the beginning of their economic growth. China is the best example, forced to raise protection standards by threats about limiting direct investments made by developed countries. Yet, with technological development, the copyright and intellectual property law is becoming less of a burden for China. Once it crosses a certain critical juncture, China will presumably join the global guardians of restrictive intellectual property protection.

For developing countries that could improve their position in the global value chains, technological advancement is not the only concern. In the pharmaceutical industry, it is also crucial for them to ensure the capability to prevent epidemics by means of statutory licensing. For them, breaking a patent monopoly means far-reaching consequences beyond merely supporting the native pharmaceutical industry that is based on production of generic medication to a greater extent than in the northernmost countries in the world.

One cannot disregard the issue of lobbying practised by the largest corporations in the world. From their point of view (at least in the context of the patent arms race, which is beneficial to them to some extent), any significant decline of invention legal protection would be problematic. Given their scale of operations, it is comparatively easy for them to build entry barriers difficult to combat within the framework of the currently binding legal regime. Thus, possible postulates of easing legal restrictions would be attacked by those companies.

However, if amendments were possible to be made, a stricter patentability regime would undoubtedly remedy the Tragedy of Intangible Abundance – most of all, as far as the requirement of non-obviousness is concerned. Imprecise provisions governing that requirement could be supplemented with a reference to 'substantial development' in a certain domain. It means for an invention to be not only obvious for a professional in a given industry branch but also to be substantial advancement (rather a notable milestone than an incremental innovation) for such a professional.

Furthermore, it would be necessary to shorten patent protection. However, one needs to bear in mind that the pace of development and life cycle of products are very much diversified in respective industries. For that reason, diversification of the maximum period of a patent protection would be worth considering for different industries. As a rule, apart from the pharmaceutical industry, it would be hard to show other industries in which protection in excess of 10–12 years would be justified. In the case of IT, much shorter protection of even four to five years would be sufficient. That mostly results from the studies (Sampat, 2018, p. 19) that prove a patent to be a strong incentive only in a few sectors (pharmacy, chemistry). That causes the patenting policy effects in respective sectors to be characterised by substantially different balances of costs and benefits. Thus, optimal patenting policy would have to be tailored to respective industries, which would, however, be very difficult to achieve – not only due to delimitation problems but most of all due to the context of international coordination of amendments in the strongly established uniform patenting system.

Shortening of patent protection would have to be accompanied by substantial acceleration of the patent application procedure. It would especially be purposeful to shorten the period between the patent application time and its publication. It could obviously not happen, which is detrimental to the procedure itself. Furthermore, it would be worth considering to add some elements that would facilitate representation of interests that are different from those represented by the applicant, to a greater extent. It is impossible to imagine a full contradictory procedure, but some elements of it would contribute to higher selectivity. As a result, the worst patents could be sieved and eliminated earlier than at the stage of litigation.

Interesting, although undoubtedly difficult to implement, is the idea of making the system of legal protection of intellectual property more flexible, as suggested by A. Bell and G. Parchomovsky (2014, pp. 234–236) who, being aware of a number of social costs arising from absolute (optionless) protection, put forward a system tailored to individual needs and requirements (self-tailored). Inventors would have the opportunity to use a number of options of protection in which the strength of entitlement would be correlated with an amount of fees payable. The authors provide examples that show the opportunities stemming from two rather extreme options that would be available on the list of choices.

First, Basics Inc., which creates fairly simple medical instruments, commercial potential of which is estimated to last four years, concurrently having very limited funds allocated to marketing, wants to raise awareness that the product information will be easy to find (instead of the standard marketing measures aimed at soliciting customers). The self-tailored one would allow to buy comparatively cheap protection for four years. However, that protection period would in such a case be defined in the course of a patent application procedure and not – as it is now – where a patent provides for protection to be sustained for a period of 20 years but an applicant may renounce from paying an annual fee for a consecutive protection period and cause a patent to expire as a result. Moreover, Basic Inc., could voluntarily limit a catalogue of possible claims in the case of property right infringement, for instance, exclusively to compensation claims. In consequence, possible court proceedings would be simpler and a possible court decision would be incorporated into a company's product publicity strategy. Thus, it would not be possible for a court to impose a ban on the sale of a product of the competitors but would award compensation, thanks to which Basic Inc. would not incur losses due to an imitator's practices but would instead benefit from an extended range of business operations.

On the opposite end of suggested arrangements, the option similar to the current system of patent protection would be available. It would be feasible for such companies that incur considerable R&D expenses and which demonstrate substantially longer product life. Then, however, such comprehensive and possibly long-lasting protection would entail much higher costs (fees).

A. Bell and G. Parchomovsky (2014, p. 236) also propose similar solutions to the copyright law. They are, however, not as revolutionary as their ideas regarding patenting. In that case it would principally mean incorporating the Creative Commons licence-based framework into commonly binding acts of law. The huge popularity of Creative Commons licences proves that authors are increasingly often interested in the law that will guarantee acknowledgement of authorship rights. They have no objection to the widespread dissemination of any work (often for commercial purposes or in the form of derivative work). Moreover, some of them have even based their business model on that diffusion, which is elaborated upon in the further part of this book.

4.1.2 Changes in patent offices

The aforementioned patent flooding causes the majority of Patent Offices to be overburdened. Those offices should be the dam protecting against patent flooding; however, they would still have to face a gigantic number of patent applications – at the very beginning at least. One may, however, expect that in the situation when Patent Offices make patenting harder, the flood of applications will be reduced, which will facilitate and ensure diligent assessment of patent application in the long run.

The analysis of the legal framework indicates that even the currently binding legal regulations allow Patent Offices to make the patenting policy stricter. Interpretation of the ambiguous requirement of non-obviousness of an invention is of utmost importance (Frakes & Wasserman, 2019). Its non-restrictiveness has been referred to in the section devoted to the causes of the Tragedy of Intangible Abundance.

According to research (Caillaud & Duchêne, 2011, p. 250), creating a statistical model for the purpose of analysing strategies of R&D companies in the context of patenting, the opportunistic approach to patenting prevails. As a result, Patent Offices are overburdened, and the number of poor patents awarded is increasing. However, it bears noting that may deal with varied states of equilibrium. Easy patenting causes patent flooding. The problem of the statistical model created by the authors arises, however, from the failure to ensure continual and cumulative process of innovation-oriented activities and patenting. That disregards the process of learning by Patent Offices on the basis of patent applications that have been submitted.

The comprehensive analysis of Patent Offices operating for 150 years in 60 countries is worth noting (Lerner, 2005). This research shows far-reaching differences. It is, however, difficult to explicitly define the tendency of the cause-effect relationship – whether a specific policy of a patent office results from economic advancement in a given country or just the opposite. Lerner has noted that in countries with larger populations and more complex economy, patent applicants have had more options at hand. From their point of view, the procedure has been more flexible – in the context of payments, protection option, or even patent application assessment timing. From the perspective of offices, much less discretional powers have been provided. Furthermore, accountability for verification of patent validity has been divided between offices and courts to a greater extent. The cited research proves significant differences between continental law and common law.

It seems, however, that (Lerner, 2005, pp. 141–142) the indicated flexibility of patenting procedures that influences innovativeness of economy in a given country may be compliant with a more restrictive understanding of the requirement of non-obviousness. Moreover, in the modern understanding of discretionary powers of the state administration, there is no real room for arbitrariness, and interpretation of ambiguous notions will not adversely impact predictability of decisions.

Lengthiness of patent award procedures is still another concern. It would undoubtedly be possible to shorten that procedure without any prejudice to diligence of the assessment process. Duration of uncertainty between submission of a patent application, its publication, and a final decision is bound to hinder companies in whose strategy a patent plays a significant role. Moreover, we are discussing such companies, the objectives of which are neither in contravention of the essence of intellectual property nor do they contribute to the increasing volume of the Tragedy of Intangible Abundance.

It is important, indeed, that such lengthy procedures are not the same problem for those who use patents in other games (non-cooperative ones) that distort the essence of legal intellectual property protection and as such contribute to the emergence of numerous negative phenomena described in this book. In such a case, the issue of time advantage and the opportunity for swift and safe commercialisation of an invention is of minor importance. There is also a fairly large group of truly innovative companies for which the opportunity to be awarded an exclusive right within a few years' time (three years following the patent claim submission, on average) makes a patent useless since fast development in some of the industries causes business potential to arise from the newest generations of products (which proves high volatility every couple of months, several months).

4.1.3 *Changes in court rulings*

Before discussing the desired changes in the practices of courts it is necessary to note that it is beneficial for system effectiveness when the bulk of cases is resolved by means of mediation. This permits avoidance of considerable costs, delays, and uncertainty that are the immanent features of court cases. Research (Ding, 2013, pp. 89–90) indicates that mediation, thanks to flexibility, provides the parties with successful solutions compliant with their interests, the majority of which go beyond any resolutions that may possibly be declared by a judge.

In the United States it is estimated that 95% of patent litigation is resolved by means of voluntary agreements instead of court decisions. At the level of the court of appeal, the mandatory mediation programme was implemented in 2005, according to which mediations were supposed to be launched before the commencement of the court hearing. Furthermore, it was required to schedule just one day for that process but attendance during mediations was not obligatory. In the first six years of implementing that pilot programme, out of 350 cases subject to mediations, 156 cases were resolved through voluntary agreements (Ding, 2013, p. 90).

One of the key questions is whether intellectual property is such a unique issue that it is beneficial to establish specialised courts to resolve disputes within that domain. The Polish government decided to do so. Its purposefulness is to some extent confirmed by studies (Biga, Możdżeń, Unpublished) that show hard to explain differences in proportions of cases heard under the ordinary procedure and writ-of-payment proceedings. The figures also show that single intellectual property cases heard by small courts take a relatively long time to be resolved. Some regularity may be spotted that such cases are heard in a systemic approach – having heard a few cases regarding intellectual property by a given court causes subsequent cases to be heard relatively efficiently.

On the other hand, however, reduction in the number of courts competent for that matter will, in a way, hinder enforcement of one's rights – in particular in the case of smaller companies. That may cause intensification of the Tragedy of Intangible Abundance since such a state of affairs will reinforce the favourable position of stronger players.

The crucial argument for specialisation would be to prove that it would contribute to better predictability of court decisions – the problem described in the previous chapter. That aspect, however, is not easy to grasp. It may be attempted to limit it exclusively to the percentage share of decisions delivered in favour of a plaintiff but that will never account for differences in the approach of intellectual property right holders towards enforceability of their rights (depending on how aggressive are their strategies). Moreover, the substantial percentage share of court decisions to reject a claim to a great extent result from non-restrictive policies of Patent Offices. As far as such cases are concerned, courts are not unpredictable but realise the function of *ex-post* control.

However, that does not mean that no postulates for court procedures can be put forward. They will, however, be universal – as they concern general drawbacks of the judicial system. Thus, within the context of intellectual property, postulates for efficient court proceedings or voluntary agreement proceedings should be put forward too.

The economic analysis of law will be crucial to improve the efficiency of court decisions, since traditional methods do not allow judges for evaluation of the real function of intellectual property in the contemporary economy. The letter of law, even if it were not limited to linguistic interpretation but included traditionally understood systemic and purpose-oriented interpretation, makes it impossible to differentiate between the nuances of utilising intellectual property for economic purposes.

4.1.4 Active innovation-oriented policy of the state

The experiences drawn from the top innovations of the twentieth century show that they could be developed thanks to considerable involvement of the state. Huge military conflicts and the cold-war competition were the obvious catalysts. That does not mean, however, that those are the only circumstances that allow state governments to realise the active innovation-oriented policy that will counteract the Tragedy of Intangible Abundance.

It should be considered how powerful and direct the interventions of the state government should be in order to stimulate innovativeness to the greatest possible and effective extent. The potential range of actions is enormous – from simple mechanism of co-financing research projects to total control over all stages – including take-over of intellectual property and its further flexible redistribution. However, it seems that far-reaching elimination of market mechanisms would not be socially beneficial. That fact, however, does not rule out the reasons and grounds for state interventions as such since the active innovation-oriented policy may be regarded as complementary to the regime of the legal protection of inventions in effective terms.

The analysis of the list of entities applying for the largest number of patents, excluding enterprises and universities, indicates the essential role of government entities. Moreover, strong representation by entities from countries such as Malaysia or India on that list undoubtedly proves effective implementation opportunities for constituents of the aforementioned model also in the developing economies.

M. Kremer (1998, pp. 1162–1163) has considered the possibility of buying out strategic patents by the government at the price equivalent to their private value fixed through bidding procedures. Benefits from such transactions arise from the difference between the social and private value of a given invention. Such a policy will obviously entail threats typical for all discretional powers. According to M. Kremer, in the case of buying out patents, such discretional powers are still not that extensive as in the case of numerous research programmes funded by the government. Such an arrangement obviously has other drawbacks too. The primary one is the difficulty with the valuation of a patent. As long as the bidding procedure – if undisturbed – may provide relevant data, it may still be affected by numerous pathological activities, such as price collusion.

The pharmaceutical industry is undoubtedly best for the government to buy out patents. Aside from the characteristic features of that market and the aforementioned social expectations, there exists a peculiar mechanism: assuming the considerable randomness of disease incidence, funding such research is a form of insurance for the society in *ex-ante* terms.

R. S. Eisenberg (1996) conducted a comprehensive review of the state interventions in the United States. Nonetheless – alarmingly too few inventions co-financed by the state budget in the period from 1957 until 1962 were used for commercial purposes. As few as only 12.4% of them were patented and only 2.7% played a meaningful role in products that were later marketed. However, that does not prejudge that an exclusive right in possession of the state government will always be less effective than interventions of a smaller scale, such as buying out non-exclusive licences.

Resistance of many social groups due to the overactive state government used to be the cause of short-term innovation paralyses. The medicinal chemistry development support programme implemented by the National Institutes of Health in the United States has been one of the most notable examples. The attempts to enforce the take-over of a substantial part of intellectual property rights by state agencies within the framework of that peculiar public-private partnership almost ended up with a unanimous boycott organised by pharmaceutical companies that were afraid of being deprived of property rights and control over tests and related deliverables.

The innovation-oriented policy undertaken by President J. Carter, although pursuing other goals, may also be regarded as relatively active in the area of inventions. Its major objective was to transfer intellectual property to small-sized enterprises and universities. The Carter Administration argued that those entities were much more motivated to commercialise innovations but they were just hindered by the lack of relevant market opportunities.

It bears noting about an interesting arrangement incorporated into the Orphan Drug Act that was adopted by the US Congress in 1983. That Act was to at least partially address the problem of insufficient benefits earned by a drug inventor within the framework of the standard patent protection due to disease rareness that translated into low forecasted demand. An orphan drug was defined to be applicable to disease or health conditions with the incidence below 200,000 individuals in the United States. By virtue of the said Act, orphan drug creators were awarded clinical trial tax incentives and other subsidies to cover the cost of creating specific drugs. Furthermore, producers received exclusive rights for a period of seven years during which no efforts were made in respect of alternative drugs of different chemical composition. Such an exclusive right could be cancelled when an entity did not provide patients with the drug or discontinued its production (Cooter & Ulen, 2016).

That Act achieved its intended goal. During 20 years before 1983 only ten orphan drugs had been awarded market approval, whereas 24 of them were issued just in 1984. During the first 15 years after the Act was approved, the number of such drugs multiplied fivefold whereas the number of other drugs only doubled. In 1993 the Act was amended to allow for patenting the subsequent second and third orphan drugs earmarked for the same disease as long as they were better than the original one under specific clinical pre-conditions (Cooter & Ulen, 2016).

4.1.5 Alternative incentives

The focus of lawyers, economists, and accountants on legal monopolies that are to guarantee creation of new intellectual property is erroneous. Empirical studies (Elkin-Koren & Salzberger, 2013, p. 69) indicate that, as a rule, the theory of incentives is undermined in business reality. Research proves that corporations do not link decisions on investing in R&D with the promise of reward, traditionally understood in intellectual property law. It seems that creating and developing innovations is profitable in the majority of cases even without extraneous classical rewards. In the context of marketing strategies, the sources of benefits are as follows: time advantage, higher production efficiency, and a privileged copyholder. Those elements are elaborated upon in the further part of this book. However, it is underlined that there are industries such as pharmaceuticals, where innovation-oriented operations could be strictly curbed or made impossible without extraneous rewards in the form of legal monopolies.

This shows that the problem is the lack of diversification of legal protection of inventions in respective industries. The nearly total unification accounts for the fact that in the majority of areas the awarded protection is too powerful – that means it generates inconveniences arising from the monopoly much above the level that is necessary to ensure the sufficient supply of innovations. Many of them would be created even without that protection. Extrapolating onto other areas the hardships that may be faced by the pharmaceutical industry in case of loosening the regime of legal protection of intellectual property makes the whole system tailored to its weakest constituent element. Apart from the difficulties arising from the diversified rules protection, there are no contraindications regarding differentiations among the industries in such a way as to make a legal monopoly become a complementary incentive – that is the one that will be available only when it is necessary to sustain development of a given branch of industry when other motivations prove insufficient.

Some domains show clear opportunities for effective incentives to encourage creative work, which are different from those arising from patent monopolies. A perfect example is that of the research community that aims at the widest possible dissemination of scientific papers. It may indeed be limited by the policy of publishers that encounter difficulties in finding alternative sources of income. However, creators themselves are ready to make financial contributions in order for their papers to be available in Open Access. It is even a common practice to negotiate the right to publish a paper on one's blog. While in the situation when some publishers attempted to prevent working papers from being published, it aroused considerable objections from the research community.

Widespread diffusion of scientific papers is to bring about numerous benefits for researchers. Some of them are hard to be quantified: the intention to impact development of scientific domain or build personal prestige (brand). However, there are also those that simply influence professional promotion or evaluation. Most important of all is the number of citations (that obviously goes up any time a paper is disseminated).

It does not mean, however, that indignation aroused by unauthorised copying is unknown in academia. It may be well exemplified by the history described by Joseph Stiglitz in his paper 'Economic Foundations of Intellectual Property Rights' (Stiglitz, 2008, pp. 1696–1697) -

> Like most academics, I have ambivalent feelings about intellectual property, illustrated by two personal stories. About twenty years ago I received a letter from a Chinese publisher asking me to write a preface to a pirated edition of one of my textbooks. As an academic, I was enthusiastic about the idea. The motivation of much academic writing is not to make money but to influence ideas and to shape the intellectual debate. China at the time was beginning the transition to a market economy: if my book helped shape that transition in a way that enhanced its likely success in raising the living standards of more than a billion people, it would have been a major. (...) Later I was at a conference in Taiwan. At that time, I knew that intellectual property rights were not always strictly enforced there. During a break in the conference, I had a little time to go to a bookstore. As I went to the store, I had a debate in my mind about what I hoped to see when I arrived. On the one hand, there was the possibility that they had stolen my intellectual property, that they had pirated one or more of my books. As we all know, theft is a terrible thing, and stealing intellectual property is a form of theft, so that would have been terrible. The other possibility was that they had not pirated one of my books and stolen my intellectual property, that they had ignored me. As I walked to the bookstore, I came to the conclusion that being ignored is far worse than having one's property stolen, and I resolved that I would actually be much happier if they had stolen my intellectual property than if they had ignored me. When I got to the bookstore, they had in fact stolen it, and I was relieved.

Literature shows (Elkin-Koren & Salzberger, 2013, p. 65) human creativity to involve a complex matrix of motivations and incentives. For that reason, it is very much detrimental when some economists restrict incentives to just financial awards. Disregarding self-motivation arising from passion, conviction, or emotional attachment to a mission is a huge cognitive gap that may be filled-in by behavioural economics.

However, the mainstream is still dominated by the conviction that non-financial incentives to create are of marginal importance.

It is obviously out of question to suggest renouncing strictly economic incentives. That even results from the fact that creation and development of innovation in some industries is very expensive. Restricting, however, just to this category will deprive one of a number of other opportunities that, having been incorporated into a relevant strategy (Directed Diffusion), will be positively reflected in the long-term in the financial results. It is viable to achieve this only under the condition that revenue, in particular quick earnings, is not the pivotal strategic objective. The digital economy causes the business model, which used to be regarded as the only successful way, to be increasingly undermined nowadays. For that reason, falling profitability of companies does not result from 'piracy' but from too slow adaptation to the reality that enforces usage of less evident tools.

4.2 Sectoral measures

Bottom-up activities are also essential to counteract the effects of the Tragedy of Intangible Abundance. Those undertaken by respective companies constitute the subject matter of the next subchapter. Here, however, the emphasis is put on indirect level of addressing problems. The mechanisms elaborated upon here pertain to specific industries – tailored to their needs and requirements. They are undertaken in the form of voluntary agreements made between entities that – especially in telecommunications – are interested in compatibility of devices manufactured by them. That is fully comprehensible due to the networking effect that accounts for the enhancement of usability of all devices, thanks to new ones being connected.

4.2.1 Standardisation organisations and patent pools

Entering into such agreements also results from the conviction that, especially in highly innovative activities, the major developmental barrier is the market size and not the competition. Therefore, companies perceive common and joint actions as advantageous in order to expand the market in which they will compete in the future. All may benefit from the larger cake to be shared. Such actions explicitly show that in varied contexts the currently binding intellectual property law is excessively restrictive and insufficiently flexible (Blind, 2016).

The FRAND (Fair, Reasonable and Non-discriminatory) terms may serve the purpose of easing the restrictive regime of intellectual property protection. Its applicability is forced in licensing by standardisation organisations that aim at ensuring compatibility of devices manufactured by diverse companies. Those organisations implement standards defining physical and functional properties of the equipment used for building networks, communication devices as well as operating systems and software. As a result, varied manufacturers may manufacture hardware and software that will be compatible based on accepted standards.

Since creation of a standard based on intellectual property owned by one player could lead to enhancement of its position, it is necessary to *a priori* disclose technical details and licensing policy that will allow competitors to incorporate that new standard into products. Those declarations constitute an essential constituent of the analysis of social costs and benefits, which precedes the decision regarding the establishing of some standard. From a model perspective, thanks to the efforts of standardizing organisations, society should receive products from different manufacturers, which will be compatible with each other.

In the recent years the number of litigation cases regarding standards has been growing. The litigation cases mainly regard patents defined as essential for a given standard, in respect of which it is viable to award a compulsory licence in case it is groundless to award a licence based on the FRAND terms. Such a possibility is part of the regulations adopted by competent authorities accountable for standardisation processes. They mostly require essential patents and key licensing terms to be defined in the standardisation process (Treacy & Lawrance, 2008, pp. 22–23).

Patents, on which standards are based, are very valuable for their holders. They guarantee substantial revenues from licence agreements, the unit price of which cannot be too high, but the related sales volume will ensure high earnings, nonetheless. Such patents are not, however, useful for all entrepreneurs, given a company's policy. Based on patents essential for standards, competition cannot be excluded from any market – licences awarded under the FRAND terms are by and large statutory. That is in contravention of principles followed by such companies as Apple Inc., which as a rule do not award licences for the use of inventions patented by them but in the course of litigation they claim a ban on sale of competitors' products that take advantage of their intellectual property.

The essence of the FRAND terms is to prevent abuse of rights of patents, on which an industry standard is based. Undertaking exclusively *ex-post* actions would place the competition in an extremely disadvantageous position because a patent holder would enjoy an excessively strong market position. It is the crowning example how other domains of law – competition law in that case – are used for lessening the strength of legal protection arising from industrial property law. Specific tools are even provided by antitrust procedures. The necessity to reach for such tools undoubtedly confirms the thesis that the patent protection regime is too strong.

Patent pools also prove to be an interesting phenomenon – agreements between at least two entities for automatic cross-licensing of intellectual property they hold. They may take a closed-ended form, where only selected entrepreneurs are admitted or an open-ended agreement made with anyone who wants to contribute and make use of a construct. The former may arouse various controversies due to the restriction of competition, which may result in reactions by state authorities accountable for the protection of fair competition. Such strategies may entail a significant risk of sanctions mainly in the European Union. The latter form plays an essential role from the perspective of the Tragedy of Intangible Abundance because it allows to counteract excessive diffusion of property (that is referred to in the Tragedy of the Anti-commons).

According to the World Intellectual Property Organisation, a typical analysis of patent pools will follow three steps: the first stage is to examine whether technologies are complementary or substitutes, i.e. competing. This is not necessarily a straightforward process and sometimes one cannot reach clear-cut conclusions. Also, the analysis cannot be static. Pooled technologies should rather be regularly reviewed based on new developments in the relevant field of technology. In the context of standardisation, it has been suggested to differentiate between standard essential and non-essential technologies. Given that standard essential technologies are by definition also complementary, pooling arrangements of essential patents generally do not raise competitive concerns whereas pooling non-essential patents will require a detailed analysis of its potential poor anti-competitive effects (World Intellectual Property Organization (WIPO), 2014).

There are many great examples, where companies voluntarily contribute to the patent pool to make a given technology even better and eventually more popular. For example, Bluetooth patent pool. As a result, competitors have expanded the market for their individual products and services. I conducted a research at the Technology Park in Kraków (unpublished at the time of this book going into print). It revealed the popularity of the approach based on such a rule: if I sell, for example, intelligent lighting system, I am deeply interested in the popularisation of Bluetooth standard – even in favour of my direct competitors and companies from diverse industries. My biggest barrier is the size of the market – which means the overall number of Bluetooth-device users. Therefore, the more popular and better Bluetooth is, the greater opportunities I have got. Therefore, I want to contribute to this standard.

However, sometimes patent pools account for a sophisticated way to build extremely strong entry barriers for competitors. We have got examples, e.g. in biotechnology, that such bundles of patents are designed to create patent thickets. Then we do not talk about any open standard but we can use a metaphor of the minefield. This is a very harmful situation because it blocks innovation and dishonestly destroys competition. Patent thickets create legal monopolies much stronger than the institution of a patent does, which it was originally designed for.

4.2.2 *Firm as an idea*

Arrangements that are to combat the Tragedy of Intangible Abundance are most of all displayed within the framework of the intellectual movement called Open Eyes Economy. The conceptual framework of Firm as an Idea, developed by J. Hausner (Hausner, 2019; Hausner & Zmyślony, 2015), focuses on the value creation process that is unique for every enterprise. Modern economics ensures that, for this process to be effective, it must include extraneous entities (customers, competitors, and even free riders). As a result it means value co-creation that is something more than merely the creation of a common good that Kramer and Porter have referred to (Porter, Michael, Kramer, & Kramer, 2011). It is also different from corporate social responsibility since the Firm as an Idea places non-economic values in the focal point of all the enterprise's activities. Consequently and contrary to CSR, in the case of financial turmoil, it is not so easy to renounce the aforementioned non-economic values.

J. Hausner claims that

> The need to develop a new approach to value in business has its underlying micro-rationale. However, general change, which emerges on the macroeconomic level, is of utmost importance. The market economy model, in which the driving force is credit-based universal consumption and financial speculation, has led to a crisis. The turn towards production based on knowledge and creativity is becoming more and more apparent. And that is not feasible without rejecting the formula 'the business of business is business'.
>
> (Hausner, 2019, pp. 234–235)

That approach also assumes denial of opportunism in intellectual property management (for instance, not utilizing every opportunity for patenting). What needs to be emphasised is that such a change is not to result exclusively from axiological reasons. Finding an individualistic – unique and unrepeatable – way of creating a company's value in real terms will cause the fear of being copied to become of secondary importance. That allows to cut costs of intellectual property protection and divert resources to what defines the essence of competitive advantage.

J. Hausner also argues that for companies 'it will be much harder (...) to find such an environment in which expansive growth will be feasible and comparatively easy. That will also bring about reflections on the sources of a company's value and development objectives. In the new, volatile, and uncertain reality, in order to ensure stability and growth for a company it will be much more important to sustainably improve the specific process of creating value than taking every possible opportunity and advantage. Just like several decades ago companies denied 'economies of size' to accept 'economies of scope', now it is the time to shift from 'economies of opportunities' to 'economies of excellence' (Hausner, 2019, p. 235).

Firm as an Idea also takes advantage of the metaphor of islands that may create archipelagos. For many enterprises it is the only way to successfully compete with giants in respective industries and – most of all – quickly growing virtual platforms that are about to build a monopsony in many domains of life (e.g. Amazon, Booking). Single companies – islands – are usually too weak to independently deal with such large-sized entities defined as continents. Therefore, within the framework of Open Eyes Economy, a solution is to create 'bubbles of change' – the network of cooperation of companies that, on the one hand maintain their separateness, but on the other mutually influence one another with enough power to be able to design and develop as archipelagos in the long run, based on their unique ways of creating value.

However, a peculiar approach to intangible resources management is required to implement such strategies (Chen, Brem, Viardot, & Wong, 2019). That approach has been called 'Directed Diffusion' and forms the content of the subsequent part of this chapter.

4.3 Company prospects: directed diffusion

Directed Diffusion is an approach that simultaneously is one of the proposals to exit the Tragedy of Intangible Abundance (or at least to mitigate its adverse impact to a great extent) and fits into the Open

Eyes Economy movement. Their common element is the need to pursue greater openness. In order to enhance the process of co-creating value it is necessary to make available certain own resources, including intangible ones, for the purpose of utilisation.

Directed Diffusion primarily refers to intellectual property (within its broad meaning – not only within the meaning of the act of law) but many of its constituents also match other kinds of intangible resources. Directed Diffusion incorporates itself into the domain between classical intellectual property management based on legal monopolies and fully open, unconditional accessibility to those resources by unlimited numbers of entities.

Within the concept of Directed Diffusion, it is worth renouncing the intellectual property management approach of protecting it by means of restrictively constrained dissemination. For effective enterprise intellectual property management, it is required to substantially constrain the scale of utilising legal monopolies (patents, copyright in the formula of 'All Rights Reserved'). Instead of ensuring exclusiveness – which is more and more expensive and sometimes practicably impossible – it is much more beneficial to develop a company's strategy based on business models that will generate benefits arising from widespread dissemination and high popularity of a construct.

Directed Diffusion allows to build permanent foundations for enterprise development – including, most of all, the opening of opportunities for profitability in the long-run – by means of disseminating intellectual property. Within this context, corporate resources sharing is regarded as investing activity that, through providing a large group of entities with access to intellectual property, lets them be included in the process of creating and processing value based on intangible resources of an enterprise. Directed Diffusion will not always mean fully independent – unlimited, uncontrolled by the enterprise – dissemination. Its essence, however, is to pursue relatively widespread dissemination.

One needs to bear in mind that the diffusion process – by definition – cannot be fully controlled since it is based on chaotically moving elements. It can be, however, guided to a certain extent. It will mean defining at which moment certain inventions/works may be disclosed to the general public, whether it is made by means of defensive publication, trade secrets, open access, non-exclusive licence agreement, or on the grounds of the Pay What You Want system, etc. The corporate strategy of intangible resources management must, however, include further – uncontrolled to a great extent – dissemination in such a way as to take advantage of the popularity/commonness of an invention or work for the purpose of earning profits in the long term. The pivotal issues of such strategies will address the sale of complementary products and services, building trust needed to cooperate with customers and competition, influencing the development of a particular market.

Since easy, quick, almost free-of-charge copying is an immanent feature of intellectual property, many persons treat those resources as especially problematic. That results from the aforementioned dominant approach toward exclusiveness and access constraints. However, regardless of capital expenditures that have already been incurred, it is impossible to guarantee effective protection to any satisfactory degree. Thus, it is necessary to seek solutions that will turn the aforementioned immanent features of intangible resources into an opportunity and not a problem. It is necessary to find such business models that will be based on relatively widespread dissemination (which does not mean beyond any control). Within that context, easy copying will no longer be a threat but an opportunity to accelerate development.

However, that requires departure from simple arrangements based on the framework: scarcity=value, control=effectiveness. In many cases, it will mean that primary revenue streams will not come from the sale of major products or services – they will be earned from complementary business operations. On top of that, the cause-effect relationship between capital expenditures and revenue will often be less apparent and requiring long-term and medium-term perspectives to be taken into account.

It requires a shift from considering knowledge in its broad meaning in statistical terms toward a dynamic approach at least addressing economies of scale or growth of a given market. The leverage effect needs to be noted. Directed Diffusion does not, however, mean simply Open Innovations. Open Access is merely one of the recommended tools, which is effective under very specific conditions. The directed dissemination – diffusion – however, means the attempt to manage at least limited control over dissemination processes in those aspects, where it is viable and profitable.

Earlier inclusion of lawyers in the decision-making process regarding intellectual resources and the company's strategy is one of the key aspects of implementation of Directed Diffusion. Some authors (Fisher & Oberholzer-Gee, 2013, p. 159) draw attention to the fact that tentative objectives of the intellectual property management strategy should be set in cooperation between managers, creators, and lawyers. One of the benefits from such an approach is the avoidance of wasting resources due to the common aversion to risk among lawyers. At a typical organisation possessing a ready-made construct, the marketing department consults a new activity and only then receives a negative decision from the legal department. Therefore, inclusion of lawyers at an earlier stage would provide for discontinuation of numerous activities that are not safe from the legal point of view. Furthermore, it would be possible to adjust the planning phase in such a way not to renounce some activities and, instead, make them safe from the legal point of view.

Directed Diffusion is supported in views earlier represented in literature – J. Stiglitz (2008) claims that applying for legal monopolies is not the only strategy that allows an enterprise to effectively use generated intellectual property. It is also indicated that, due to increasingly visible drawbacks of legal protection, in a number of industries an alternative method of intangible resources management is gaining importance (Bessen & Meurer, 2008). In consequence, a growing number of companies do not consider easy copying, which is the immanent feature of intellectual property, to be exclusively a threat (Andergassen, Nardini, & Ricottilli, 2017). In those terms they perceive the opportunity to accelerate the emergence of a new market, widening opportunities of selling complementary goods and services or take advantage of such business models that are based on the networking effect.

According to the studies conducted in the United States (Lallement, 2017) and data compiled in the Community Innovation Survey (CIS) in other parts of the world, the rate of return on informal methods (time advantage, trade secrets, products complexity) is assessed much higher than traditional tools. The intensity with which legal tools are used is affected by aspects such as enterprise size or the innovation's stage of development.

Clearly, Directed Diffusion is not a universal strategy. Its effectiveness depends on a number of factors – primarily on the type of industry. The pharmaceutical industry, that is most often referred to by defenders of the patenting system, will much more often need a legal monopoly to yield a satisfactory rate of return compared to software creators. The pharmaceutical industry enjoys access to the mechanisms of building a competitive advantage. It is well exemplified even by medications, the patent for which has expired, but in spite of accessibility of cheaper substitutes, many consumers accustomed to a specific trademark (for instance, Aspirin) may be inclined to pay more for a product they know well. It obviously does not provide such a strength as a patent-based monopoly does but it is free from constraints – such as time constraints.

It should be emphasized that Directed Diffusion does not assume total renunciation of patenting but only rejects regarding it as the only way or the default way. Preferring a patent to other tools may be in numerous cases easily explained by means of the bonus system at an enterprise or reliance on classical methods of innovation assessment. However, it is in the interest of an organisation to at least consider the alternative methods elaborated on in the following part of this book. What is important is that only some of them may be considered as patent substitutes in the understanding that they provide protection/exclusiveness in a different way (trade secrets, software-as-a-service). Many of them, on the other hand, are based on widespread dissemination that paves the way for revenues earned outside core activities.

4.4 Benefits from directed diffusion

Even in industries in which traditional forms of intellectual property protection prove effective, the majority of patents do not bring benefits and must be regarded as sunk costs. Withdrawal – namely renouncing the payment of subsequent patent maintenance fees – allows, however, to save only part of patenting costs. The majority of them are incurred at the stage of patent application (patent purity search, description preparation, registration).

4.4.1 Reduction of intellectual property maintenance costs

The need to verify the intellectual property management strategy that is often based on legal monopolies is noted even in the chemical industry, which, besides the pharmaceutical industry, is the one that desires patents most.

Since 1990, businesses are conducting IP audits. IP audit is one of the emerging IPM practices, which helps managers to understand the potential IP along with IP owned by an organisation. 'If we know it, we can manage it,' considering this mantra organisations are performing IP audit though it is not statutory. Dow Chemicals is the first organisation to conduct its first organisation-wide audit of IP assets in 1994. Dow achieved an immediate savings of USD 50 million in taxes and maintenance fees on unneeded patents, and earnings in licensing revenues skyrocketed from USD 25 million to more than USD 125 million. IBM earned USD 1.7 billion in revenues from patent licensing in 2000 alone and Texas Instruments earned USD 500 million. It has been reported that 67% of US organisations own technology assets that they fail to exploit (assessed at between USD 115 billion to USD 1 trillion).

About USD 100 billion are tied up in an idle innovation within the IP portfolios of big companies.

(Gargate, Siddiquee, & Wingkar, 2019)

It is often forgotten that intellectual property maintenance costs include costs of rights enforcement claims brought before a court, though if the case is won, the substantial amount of costs may be recovered (Grzegorczyk, 2020). The aforementioned high unpredictability of that type of proceedings accounts for the statistical success in every second case. Moreover, the opportunity to apply for cost reimbursement if one wins the case before a court is strictly constrained in many legal systems.

The cost of time is often disregarded but taken into account by start-up owners. For the majority of them the choice is apparently obvious in the case of the dilemma of assigning resources (financial, time) either to legal protection application (even believing in possibly fully effective protection) or to product development in order for the next product generation to bring much more benefits for consumers than the generation that has been possibly copied by competition. This is obviously connected with building a strategy based on time advantage, which is an increasingly dominant approach, especially in the digital economy.

4.4.2 Better opportunities to sell complementary goods and services

Changes occurring in the economy mean that companies often have to search for sources of revenue beyond their traditionally understood core activities. In fixed assets-based economy, such a change is most visible in the case of petrol stations that, due to strong competition, may only set minor profit margins on fuel sales while substantial profits are earned from more and more developed petrol station convenience stores and coffee shops in which, as a rule, profit margins are as high as several hundred per cent.

That phenomenon will spread onto other areas. Software creators will more often provide software for free in order to earn from after-sale services, tailored cloud services, or customisation services towards the needs of a specific organisation. Musicians more often will provide their records for free, counting on concert ticket sales and revenue from sales of authorised souvenirs for which consumers are inclined to pay exorbitant sums of money (Krueger, 2019). So, the logic is reversed, for in the past even a sold-out music tour yielded huge earnings but was nonetheless considered as a tool to promote the album. Today vice versa, albums are 'leaflets' encouraging to buy concert tickets that become more and more significant sources of income for musicians.

If we look closer at such phenomena, they are not entirely new. For years, similar strategies have been implemented by manufacturers of printers. The actual devices were very cheap whereas disposable parts (printing ink, cartridges) were horrendously expensive. After-sale services also account for a substantial part of profits earned by automotive companies. History knows numerous ways of commercialising popularity where primary business is run for free or very cheaply and what is complementary in theory, is the best source of income in practice.

4.4.3 Impact on market development

The market development impact is an argument that cannot be ignored when the intangible resources management strategy is put together. In many cases an under-developed market is the most serious barrier for business scalability. Within this context, the opportunity to accelerate market development, and most of all, guiding its direction, may be crucial from the point of view of long-term profitability. Therefore, in the open knowledge community it is much more beneficial to be a co-participant than a free rider (Foray, 2013, p. 14).

Tesla's decision to open up all the electric car-related patents it owns is a peculiar strategy that follows this mindset. On the one hand, it may be perceived in the context of sticking to the convictions for 'freedom of knowledge and openness'. On the other hand, however, in that particular case it has a deep pragmatic and business sense. That movement is to contribute to acceleration of electromobility popularisation, which is beneficial for Tesla even if some pieces of the 'cake' are taken by competitors. The weakness of the electric vehicle battery charging infrastructure is currently one of the largest barriers to E. Musk's business development. Even if Tesla itself is actively involved in building it, providing a sufficiently high number of charging stations will be impossible. After successful popularisation of electric cars, more entities will be interested in investments in charging stations, which will be beneficial to all the manufacturers, and most of all Tesla as the market leader.

It is important to remember that in the knowledge economy value is not built on scarcity. Currently the value of knowledge is proportionate to the size of the market in which it may be sold. Other authors (Oleksak & Adams, 2010, p. 6) also draw attention to the fact that knowledge in itself is not a ready-made economic good yet. It may become one when 'it addresses a problem in a way that people will be inclined to pay for'. If such a problem has already been identified, its value is limited to the greatest extent by the number of persons who may need the solution. Therefore, there are no physical constraints, only the demand is limited due to market size.

4.4.4 Success stories of open approach to intellectual property

Directed Diffusion is not a totally new model that only now must be tested in business. On the contrary, it is an attempt to build a conceptual framework based on observations of activities undertaken by enterprises in various industries, that – for diverse reasons – have resolved to represent a more open approach to their intellectual property management.

It is worth considering the example of Volvo that developed three-point safety belts (lap safety belts, similar to those currently used in aeroplanes, used to be fastened in cars). Test results proved them to be much more effective in terms of health and life safety. Volvo opened up that patent free-of-charge to all its competitors. Such a decision could have seemed to be ethically appropriate but crazy from the business perspective. The subsequent analyses, however, proved that it in the long-run prospects it was also a marvellous decision from the business point of view. In consequence, Volvo reinforced its image as a safety leader. It also accounted for its potential customers' conviction that economic results would not be pursued at the cost of human life or health concerns (which was also evidenced by Volvo's shared care for drivers and passengers of competitive brands). A number of more technically advanced safety systems are obviously protected by exclusive rights owned by Volvo. But that is just the essence of Directed Diffusion – it is not all about unconditional disclosure of all one owns.

Fiat Mio, an urban car design developed by Fiat in a totally openness-based approach, is another example from the automotive industry. The whole design dossier, which had been developed with great involvement from customers, was available by means of Creative Commons licences.

The market of mobile device operating systems is worth being analysed, too. When in 2007 Google showed interest in developing a technologically advanced system design that would be available to all free-of-charge – and on top of that respective device manufacturers and operators would be free to modify it – that decision was incomprehensible to many. It, however, turned out that Google managed to dominate the market). Similarly to Volvo, it was not just a mere mission, a public service, at all. Google incorporated its key services as default ones into the system (the browser, e-mail accounts, maps, documents) and further has earned substantial income from commissions on the sale of third party applications in Google Play Store.

Apple, which is famous for its closed-ended approach to intellectual property protection (for instance, in the case of infringement it does not usually claim compensation but demands a ban on sale of competitors' products, or does not consent to macOS or iOS systems licensing for the benefit of other manufacturers), also had to learn a more open approach. The first iPhone did not provide for installing any other additional applications, and if it were not for having eased those limitations, iPhone would not have made such a spectacular market success. Apple has created an application store in which games and software made by even major competitors are available (upon successful verification). That decision has not only increased iPhone's usability but has also allowed Apple to earn gigantic commissions.

Furthermore, the approach referred to in the Directed Diffusion is not limited to the largest companies. As my studies on start-ups at the Technological Park in Kraków have indicated, those small-sized companies are still less interested in developing their business operations based on patents or copyrights with 'All Rights Reserved'. In some cases, the lack of will to patent results from the lack of funds to cover the cost of the patent application procedure. In some cases, however, those companies could afford the costs but they know that they would not be able to afford the costs of possible patent protection maintenance in case it is infringed in distant countries (for Polish start-ups American lawyers' hourly rates are prohibitive).

The conducted surveys have shown that the majority of those companies' top managers do not regard legal monopolies as needed for business purposes. That mostly results from the lengthiness of procedures at Patent Offices. Start-ups prefer building their competitive advantage on time advantage – 'the moment someone manages to copy/imitate my product, I shall already have it upgraded to the second- or third-generation product'. Time advantage will be presented in a greater detail in the following part of this chapter.

Start-ups in Kraków also appreciate the open source movement. The majority of them contribute to it to a little extent. They, however, do not share the opinion that a construct accessibility within the framework of the Open Access will not make it possible to derive financial benefits from it because key customers will need customised implementation (product-tailored) and after-sale services. So, software creators will be the obvious choice as providers of such services. Their product knowledge is a sufficient competitive advantage. Making something available via Open Access is a good way to publicise a construct and encourage other programmers to create compatible constructs (that will additionally enhance usability of the basic software).

From the point of view of the surveyed enterprises, the approach defined as Directed Diffusion is something natural that does not need further incentives to be taken advantage of. However, they are also affected by the Tragedy of Intangible Abundance since they are afraid that, after having developed a sufficiently large scale of business operations, they may be targeted by companies that will attempt to damage them by means of unpredictable court proceedings. Until now, however, none of the surveyed companies has experienced that. Moreover, they are consistent in regarding legal protection of intellectual property as disadvantageous. They are also consistently reluctant to sue other entities in case their intellectual property right is infringed.

4.5 Directed diffusion: instruments

As it has already been mentioned, Open Access is just one tool that may be used for the purpose of implementing Directed Diffusion. It is hard to imagine Open Access to be the only standard. In some of the industries (chemical, pharmaceutical industry) there are serious, objective difficulties with renouncing patents. Furthermore, a number of specific cases in other industries support the argument for some control over information dissemination.

4.5.1 Open access

As a rule, the Open Access may constitute a good strategy in the following categories of cases:

1   Finding a method for widespread supply of complementary goods and services
2   Reliance on existing market power (e.g. a recognisable trademark)
3   Treating Open Access as a temporary strategy to accelerate market development
4   Activities enhancing company image, covering a specific (narrow) extent of business operations

4.5.1.1 Finding a method for widespread supply of complementary goods and services

Businesses based on earning revenue from complementary goods and services are nothing new in economics. Usually, they encounter some constraints arising from costs of manufacturing or producing a primary product, which do not approximate to zero. For instance, printer manufacturers sell many very cheap models (though they cannot give them away for free) in order to earn revenue from expensive disposable parts, while in the case of intellectual property, the marginal cost of manufacturing another copy usually approximates to zero. Thus, one may provide something for free – significantly arousing interest among buyers, creating larger opportunities to sell complementary goods and services.

4.5.1.2 Reliance on existing market power (e.g. a recognisable trademark)

That approach is applied by the Italian Arduino Company that manufactures simple electronic gadgets. The complete technical dossier of those devices is available in the Internet by means of open licences. Thus, they are possible to be copied independently. It is the brand, a registered trademark, that allows Arduino to build competitive advantage. That trademark is allowed to be used exclusively on devices manufactured by Arduino. For many consumers that guarantees quality which is the incentive encouraging them to buy devices directly from the inventor- manufacturer (Oleksak & Adams, 2010, p. 15).

4.5.1.3 Treating Open Access as a temporary strategy to accelerate market development

In case when the market size is the barrier for business development, it is worth easing competitors' business operations in order for them to support us in enhancing the market. Such activities are to enlarge the cake to be shared and benefited by all the players – regardless of the ultimate market share they will enjoy in result of competition driven by other factors. That strategy was taken advantage of by Tesla.

4.5.1.4 Activities enhancing company image, covering a specific (narrow) extent of business operations

Open Access may be used for marketing purposes. Consumers usually appreciate such 'selflessness', and in some industries (e.g. programming), it is even the pre-condition to make a construct be treated seriously. Within this context, Toyota's decision to open up 24,000 hybrid drive-related patents maybe taken into consideration.

4.5.2 *Defensive publications*

Defensive Publications are very useful tools in case when an enterprise does not fear that a construct may be used by competitors as long as no third party is able to deny its use to the owner. That is mainly the case when an inventor believes himself to be capable of acting more successfully than the competitors, at least due to the effect of scale, recognisable brand, and controlled product ecosystem. Then the competitive advantage is sufficient and does not have to be reinforced by legal monopolies.

Reduction of costs of patenting and maintaining patent protection is the major advantage of defensive publications. It is sufficient to publish a description of an invention in order for it to become a constituent of the state of the art, which therefore assures the impossibility of fulfilling the criterion of novelty – one of the requirements of patentability. In effect, no one will be in a position to submit the related patent application form to the patent office. Such a defensive publication does not require any financial outlays, and contrary to trade secrets, does not bear any risk that could arise from the fact that another entity will independently come into possession of an invention or through uncontrolled information disclosure, and will subsequently obtain the exclusive right that will exclude its actual inventor from using it.

Weakening competition is paradoxically still another advantage arising from a defensive publication. When an invention cannot be patented, it means that no one can use it for the purpose of building any competitive advantage. That approach is used by the processor manufacturing giant – Intel. It patents exclusively key functionalities of a new sub-assembly. It also publishes defensively in order to discourage competitors from seeking around the patent, solutions similar to the primary product are published defensively. That substantially combats inclination to imitate. As in practice the boundaries of a patent are much wider because one may legitimately create similar constructs – to those referred to in the defensive publication – but one cannot use it for building a competitive advantage over other imitators. Therefore, it is much harder to assume a satisfactory revenue, given the strong pressure on price reduction down to the amount equivalent to the marginal costs, the more so as Intel itself at the same time offers a better construct that has already been patented.

Small and medium-sized companies also use the strategy of defensive publishing (Brant & Lohse, 2013, p. 15). It most often does not, however, accompany the procedure of patenting the major innovation but the procedure of maintaining it as a trade secret. It is a somewhat risky strategy because kindred constructs published defensively may guide competitors to that particular secret and confidential construct. On the other hand, it helps to build the impression that a given area is principally either in the public domain or is occupied by an excessively dominant position of a major player. However, due to high costs of patenting, smaller companies are forced to undertake such risky measures. As in the case of smaller companies, even if they possess sufficient resources to obtain patent protection, they are often also aware that they lack sufficient funds to defend the received patent in the case of litigation – especially when infringement is made in a different country. Costs of possible litigation are often more than the costs of patenting and patent maintenance. Therefore, trade secrets accompanied by defensive publications are the only way.

4.5.3 Time advantage and first copy holder privilege

Time advantage allows an innovative enterprise to obtain a certain pool of benefits even should the law not protect intellectual property, something often forgotten, since the managers focus on obtaining and enforcing legal protection. The scale of such benefits varies depending on the industry and opportunities for quick imitation. In case when the manufacturing process is known and it is relatively easy to manufacture a product (printing, for example), the first copy holder privilege is relatively insignificant. In a reverse situation, when complicated changes are necessary to adjust the manufacturing process to a new product (e.g. microprocessors), the time advantage assures much greater benefits. In such a case, fast pace of development makes several-year-old constructs obsolete enough for an innovator not to face substantial losses on their unauthorised use because newer constructs exclusively carry commercial potential.

However, even in industries that are tougher from that point of view, it is still possible to discount the time advantage to a satisfactory extent. The example of Aspirin shows that an innovator's market share is much larger than the imitators' even if they offer perfect substitutes at substantially lower prices (Boldrin & Levine, 2008, p. 127). Therefore, it is more effective to use time advantage in which the original monopolistic price substantially approaches the marginal cost (under the competition pressure after the patent expiry) in order to continue generating surplus. Thus, after substitutes have emerged it is still possible to ensure the competitive advantage, provided that a registered trademark has increased its value within the pre-imitation period.

Research shows (Boldrin & Levine, 2008, p. 141) that substantial income is earned at the beginning period of product or service availability. In the case of writers, 80% of book sales are achieved within the first three months. It is noticeable that consumers can pay much more for fast access. The cited example is of an industry in which discounts of several dozen per cent are very common only after a couple of months following a product release.

Online store delivery forms chosen by buyers allow to arrive at similar conclusions. A considerable number of them are ready to pay even multiple of basic delivery term cost in order to receive the parcel a couple of days earlier. Amazon, which had not offered Prime Packages at the beginning of its business operations (including free delivery), once started the service, reported much higher popularity of the option of delivery in 24 hours for $2.99 as compared to the standard delivery in two days for $1.99 and the longest delivery term – from three to seven days for $0.99 (Boldrin & Levine, 2008, p. 141). It is a similar case with crowdfunding that shows huge interest of consumers in early access. They are inclined to pay more in advance accepting a higher risk of project failure or disappointment for the option of a pre-premiere delivery.

Literature (Boldrin & Levine, 2013, p. 10) gives an example of the iPhone, which came to market on 29 June 2007, and exemplifies substantial benefits that may be derived from time advantage. The first real competition – HTC Dream based on Android – emerged over a year later – on 22 October 2008. At that time Apple did not block competition by means of patents (such a strategy was adopted only after 2010). Notwithstanding that Apple achieved iPhone a sales volume of over 5 million in the first year and 25 million – in the consecutive year. Within that period Android-based competitors achieved only a sales volume of 7 million. That means such an innovative product could bring about substantial benefits for creators although legal monopolies were not used.

4.5.4 Pay what you want

The Pay What You Want (PWYW) model is one of underappreciated ways of intellectual property dissemination. It comes with a price that is not fixed by a vendor (in some options a minimal price is established). It is a method perfectly fitting intellectual property, whose marginal cost approximates to zero. Within this context, in the case of distribution of software, for instance, seasonal price reduction of up to 90% of the original price is no surprise, at all. It surely is the aim to maximise profit by gaining consumers for whom the original price is too high and they are inclined to wait for a special bargain, concurrently earning higher incomes from customers for whom the original price is affordable and they are ready to pay that price for immediate access.

The PWYW model is partly based on similar assumptions – namely, on the intention to maximise profits on the basis of understanding diverse inclination of customers to pay. However, the reference to other categories of value is still another important element. It is an explicit denial of perceiving people in terms of Homo Oeconomicus. If it were not for a wider axiological context, one would not be able to expect anyone to pay a higher amount than the minimal price. The PWYW success stories, however, show that especially in the domain of fine arts, though not the only, consumer behaviour is impacted by a number of stimuli other than economic ones. It is mostly all about acknowledgement, respect, appreciation, feeling of duty (being something different from restrictive obligation).

Furthermore, examples of success stories may be found at various levels of professional activities. Street musicians represent the most common and oldest implementation of the PWYW. They perform having no guarantee of being paid for. As a matter of fact, the majority of listeners are free-riders, but those who decide to pay for the experience do so sufficiently compensating the musician for the 'loss', which is proven by the continual popularity of that type of earning a living. In popular spots local authorities have to regulate that type of performance.

At the other pole of professionalism is the band Radiohead, which released the album 'In Rainbows'. Fans downloading that album turned out to be willing to pay the price similar to the standard price earned by musicians, less the distribution costs. Losses, caused by individuals downloading the record for a lower price, were covered by individuals paying more. The PWYW model allows wealthier fans to give some kind of a tip – to express special acknowledgement of an artist's creativity. They are deprived of that opportunity in terms of traditional distribution.

The PWYW model also brings about a number of image building benefits. It may even be an effective marketing tool. The promotion of 'Pantera Bread' American restaurant chain, which sold one of its sandwiches in that way at one of its restaurants in St. Louis, may serve as an example of actions that considerably contributed to higher popularity of the company, as the campaign was widely discussed in the media and generated sizeable interest due to its uniqueness. The model under consideration was first used as early as in 1984 at Annalakshmi Restaurant in Malaysia. The PWYW model gained high popularity also in the software market where it is used as a bonus that a user of free software may give to its creator.

4.5.5 Trade secrets

Trade secrets constitute an underappreciated alternative to patents. In many cases they may be much more effective, particularly in the long-term perspective. Their advantages include:

– no fees payable for application for and maintenance of protection (patent fees, patent attorney fees) – trade secrets are protected automatically based on the regulations governing prevention of unfair competition
– no administrative protection time constraints
– no requirement to describe in detail and publicise a construct (which is the case with patent descriptions).

Disadvantages of trade secrets include:

– the need to adjust business operations to conditions of high confidentiality (workflow, employment contracts, actual operations, etc.)
– the risk of patenting a construct by independently operating competitors and, as a result, levying a ban on using a construct.

Studies conducted in the United States show, however, that American R&D staff and managers regard trade secrets as a more effective protection than patents. Effectiveness of the former is assessed to account for 51% and the latter for 23–35% (Boldrin & Levine, 2008, p. 167). Authors also pay attention to the fact that in many cases an inventor is not self-motivated to be protected by a patent. It is especially the case with a developing market. Then the risk of imitating is comparatively low. In such situations a hasty decision to enter the market would carry a higher risk – much higher than a typical risk that is characteristic for patent racing. However, delayed patenting creates incentives for competitors to develop and test various constructs. That also creates a space for making tentative steps that will facilitate final decision-making in respect of patenting and possible commercialising, that will be the easiest for the leader – actual inventor (Boldrin & Levine, 2008, p. 167). In other words: maintaining indirect constructs confidential in the case of high uncertainty about demand will make it possible to shift a part of the risk onto competitors without the danger that competitors would seize potential benefits.

Within the context of business secrets it is essential to differentiate between tacit knowledge and explicit knowledge. Tacit knowledge is not transferable. It is reflected in specific constructs but even without building any barriers it cannot be perfectly copied and used elsewhere efficiently. Moreover, it plays a significant role in creating strategic advantages of an enterprise. It means that, to a great extent, using business secrets is completely natural, fully effective, and does not generate any costs. One needs to bear in mind that trade secrets not only include the approach that is alternative to patenting, but also comprise know-how components that 'surround' a patent or may constitute competitive advantage also once a patent expires. This encompasses the whole knowledge of an organisation, that makes it most effective when it is used in the organisation that is its author.

That thesis may be confirmed by the most famous inventions in history. For example, James Watt was involved in the creation and dissemination of engines based on his construct even after the steam engine patent had expired. It may also be exemplified in more contemporary terms as the automotive industry proves when Japanese and European corporations fully emerged in the United States, the American manufacturers took longer to catch up with competitors' combustion efficiency rates. Honda, Toyota, Fiat, and Rover were top leaders for years successfully competing with General Motors and Ford in that respect, although numerous relevant constructs were longer protected by patents and the very engine construction design was impossible to be kept confidential, given the mass manufacturing and sales (Boldrin & Levine, 2008, p. 163).

The visible aberration of the current system of intellectual property protection is the attempt made by many entrepreneurs to combine trade secrets and patents by means of ambiguous patent claims. Such practice is feasible as a result of low quality of patent application assessment by Patent Offices. It is often indicated that it is impossible to retrace an invention by reading a patent description. Therefore, it does not result in crucial knowledge dissemination that is incorporated into the model framework of the patenting system. One of the more prominent examples is that of the patented fifth-dimensional information transmission (US Patent 6,025,810) that cannot be retraced on the basis of the existing state of the art and background knowledge. Such use of trade secrets does not only contribute to enhancing the Tragedy of Intangible Abundance (instead of mitigating its impact) but it actually mocks the intellectual property law. Paradoxically it may, however, have a positive outcome since the public opinion needs vivid absurdities in order to initiate deeper changes.

4.5.6 Alternative business models

The Tragedy of Intangible Abundance proves that it is profitable to search for benefits based on widely understood complementary goods and services instead of narrowly understood commercialisation of a construct. It is often necessary even to go beyond those categories just like it was the case with petrol stations that developed shops, fast food, and cafes to compensate low profit margins on fuel sales. Nowadays it is a rule that non-core activities are the source of higher income because they are based on products sold with immensely greater profit margins. Thus, in the case of petrol stations, fuelling is just to attract a consumer.

The very knowledge regarding possible innovation – being an intangible resource too – allows innovation-oriented activities to become highly profitable for their holder under certain conditions. It is obvious that the largest resource of the aforementioned knowledge is in possession of the entity creating an invention, which provides the entity with tools that are unavailable for anyone else. Moreover, within a framework of a successful strategic plan, patenting (and the consequent access constraints) would adversely impact the effectiveness of a non-obvious business plan. Such a strategy may be exemplified (Foray, 2013, pp. 21–22) by an innovation that comes in the form of using volcanic dust for enhancing parameters of concrete. With the addition of volcanic dust, the durability and water resistance of concrete are improved. The entity that has developed that novelty may take advantage of that foreground knowledge for investing purposes instead of patenting it and subsequently combating unauthorised use of the patented invention. The new construct will cause the demand for volcanic dust to rise considerably, which will translate into the corresponding increase in the price for that resource. Early purchase of those resources will ensure a very high rate of return – and it will be still higher the more popular the invention becomes.

The software industry is the area in which business models that are far from traditional have gained highest popularity. It is more and more common and typical for that industry to offer applications free-of-charge with the option to purchase technical support. That is especially typical for more advanced software used for professional applications. That phenomenon results from recognition of certain developments:

1   Professionals, for whom software is essential for their job, are inclined to incur even relatively high costs in order to enjoy its undisturbed use.
2   The company that has created a given piece of software enjoys an enormous competitive advantage over others – when it comes to professional technical support it knows the software best (including the best potential to customise it for specific customers); it is thus in a way, a monopolist, which also creates the opportunity to dictate high prices.
3   Amateurs are not inclined, and sometimes they cannot simply afford to cover the costs of such a software licence. However, the more of them get familiar with a specific software, the more probable it is to be obligated to pay for the use of that software in the case of a larger scale of operations.
4   The smaller the financial barriers to education, the more popular the software becomes at training courses, workshops, and university classes. Graduates accustomed to a specific construct will put pressure on possible employers to be able to use (commercially) the software they are most familiar with.

Understanding the above means that using such a software program for the purpose of Directed Diffusion – namely widespread dissemination based on free licences for educational or other non-professional purposes, and under some conditions the availability for small business and in extreme cases for everyone free-of-charge – will not prejudice the chances of earning profits. As profits may be earned on the basis of paid technical support, training courses, integration with other (traditionally shared) modules, etc.

The freemium model (majority of functionalities are available for free, just premium components are paid for) is also used by many bloggers. They share their knowledge substantially in the form of materials available free-of-charge in the Internet. Then, over time, they start to offer training courses/books/individual consultation to their community. They do not usually hide that the extent of paid services is very much similar to what has already been made public. Several additional components, however, are sufficient to make such actions produce amazing results.

The scale of such successes is undoubtedly the result of the intention of loyal readers to return a favour. The Patronite platform works on the basis of that mechanism, where content viewers agree to support the Internet creator (even if it is not the pre-condition to gain access to some premium content). Individuals who regard one's activities as especially valuable want, for instance, to sustain or equip a creator with new devices (so that a creator does not have to undertake other activities to earn a living and could focus on delivering new content). That approach, which is hard to justify within standard economic reasoning (due to the fear of too strong free-rider problem), in practice is more and more common and shows that restrictive legal measures are often unnecessary to earn money from intellectual property.

Within the context of non-obvious exploitation of intangible resources it is worth referring to the revolution in financial services during the 1970s. The need to eliminate intermediaries (disintermediation) was noticed then. That same lesson may today be learnt in creative branches of industry. The development of the Internet has more often proved that intermediaries between an artist and a viewer, a programmer and a customer are unnecessary (especially in the case of emerging and less popular projects). Popularity of self-publishing, independent production of records, and distribution of software by means of independent platforms provides for substantial reduction of prices paid by end-users and concurrent increase in profits earned by authors themselves.

In traditional distribution models they may usually count only on a few per cent share in the price paid by a consumer. That means that only very high sales volume will allow to earn a living. Thus, it is a huge entry barrier that may be impossible to be challenged in the case of more niche projects. Moreover, a high end price (arising from intermediaries' profit margins) will stimulate unauthorised information exchange that is usually called 'piracy'. The more frequent the phenomenon is, the smaller the sales volume and the smaller profits creators earn.

The Internet's technical capacity, especially peer-to-peer software, makes intermediaries simply redundant in so many cases. The blockchain revolution may even accelerate that process. Creators have also been provided with a tool used for easy, dynamic pricing policy in respect of exploitation of their intellectual property, dissemination tracing, and even partial control over the diffusion area (obtained in the same way as the upper limit on the number of Bitcoins that may be mined, that is known in advance).

A stricter control over the distribution process also means that an author may exercise personal copyrights to a greater extent. Economists excessively focus on the copyright in terms financial rewards because the rights of the author are as important (if not the most important rights) as they are non-transferrable and are not time-constrained. Successful enforcement of such rights as fame and reverence for work is much easier in a process controlled by the author. Moreover, it is done without any prejudice to property rights that will not be exercised in a standard form (licensing, property right transfer) but instead a creator will be in a position to make money on own works in a less obvious manner. In the above circumstances it is possible to use very dynamic arrangements, which may be very useful in the context of reacting to the price elasticity of demand. Such measures, in the case of intellectual property, dissemination of which generates marginal costs that approximate to zero, provide for great opportunities to undertake adaptive activities, of which the aforementioned PWYW system is the most vivid form.

4.5.7 Non-exclusive licences

Non-exclusive licences are not only to be used for earning revenue. Another role they play, that is often disregarded, is to discourage imitation and to curb the scale of the phenomenon called 'searching around a patent' (Fisher & Oberholzer-Gee, 2013, p. 162). From the point of view of a creator who is a patent holder, two situations are possible:

1   The granted patent has relatively clear boundaries and the effective intellectual property rights enforcement system is in place, so possible imitators will focus on searching around a patent – they will seek a construct that will go beyond the boundaries of a specific patent. In principle, that means denial of an optimal arrangement and opting for a worse product. Its creation is undoubtedly easier and cheaper than the creation of the original invention; however, it is not costless anyway – it also requires some capital expenditures.

2   The patent boundaries are very ambiguous and there is no effective intellectual property rights enforcement system in place – so imitators will straightforwardly copy the patented invention (or almost straightforwardly make minor diversionary alterations). Their costs will then be very low. From the consumer perspective, imitated products will provide similar usability, so the creator of

the original invention will not be able to develop a competitive strategy based on quality, either.

The second situation in principle denies the purposefulness of maintaining such a patent. However, the first situation is worth analysing. In that case it is necessary to define an appropriate amount of licence fees that must arise from two values: costs of imitation and diminishing usability (taken into consideration in the context of price elasticity of demand for a given product) determined by the given patent boundaries. On top of that one needs to keep a safety legal margin that to some extent will mean a high risk of after-effect. In consequence, by the accurate calculation of licence fees, a licensee will generate revenue for an inventor (by means of licence fees paid) instead of being an imitator putting pressure on the reduction of the price of the original product. The networking effect is still reinforcing the positive outcome of such an arrangement as it also results in a rising value of each copy due to dissemination of fully compatible goods or services.

Microsoft and IBM used to take advantage of non-exclusive licensing in the last decades of the twentieth century. Contrary to them, Apple did not license its software to any other manufacturer. As a result, in 2003 Apple's personal computer market share amounted only to 1.9% (Fisher & Oberholzer-Gee, 2013, p. 163). If it were not for the mobile device revolution, relying solely on computer sales would not have allowed Apple to survive.

Licensing is profitable not only when competitors are able to use an innovation more effectively than its creator, but it may also serve the purpose of expanding the market and increasing the demand for the innovator's other products. Literature (Fisher & Oberholzer-Gee, 2013, p. 165) refers to the example of Monsanto – one of the top global players in the field of agricultural biotechnology. The enormous power of that company is derived from two inventions. The first one is Roundup (its patent expired in 2000) – a powerful herbicide. The other ones are genetically modified seeds that allow to use Roundup at a longer time interval without any damage to crops. The first generation of that innovation has not been protected by any patent since 2014. The second generation's patent expires in 2020.

As the cited author notes (Fisher & Oberholzer-Gee, 2013, pp. 165–166)

> Monsanto could have used its patents to exclude competitors from the rapidly growing industry of genetically modified crops (the most important application of which involves soybeans). Perhaps surprisingly, it has not. Instead, it has entered into licensing

agreements of two sorts. First, it has granted licenses (on reasonable terms) to several hundred seed companies, authorising them to develop and sell seeds embodying the 'Roundup Ready' technology. Second, it has granted licences to its principal rivals (DuPont [Pioneer Hi-bred], Bayer, Syngenta, Dow AgroSciences, and BASF) to combine the Roundup Ready genes with other modified genes to produce seeds with multiple advantages: drought resistant, insect resistance, and so forth. Adoption of this strategy has benefitted Monsanto in three ways. First, by capitalising on the production capacity and marketing abilities of other firms, Monsanto spread the technology faster than it could have done on its own, and thus not only increased total industry revenues (much of which Monsanto is able to garner through license fees), but also corroded popular resistance to genetically modified crops, which has been based in part on unfamiliarity. Second, the 'technological lock-in' achieved through licensing seems to have enabled Monsanto to engage in a novel form of 'evergreening'— the popular term for extending the effective duration a patent or other IP right.

References

Andergassen, R., Nardini, F., & Ricottilli, M. (2017). Innovation diffusion, general purpose technologies and economic growth. *Structural Change and Economic Dynamics, 40*, 72–80.

Bell, A., & Parchomovsky, G. (2014). Reinventing copyright and patent. *Michigan Law Review, 113*, 231–278.

Bessen, J., & Meurer, M. J. (2008). *Patent Failure* (pp. 1–347). Princeton, NJ and Oxford: Princeton University Press.

Blind, K. (2016). The impact of standardisation and standards on innovation. In *Handbook of Innovation Policy Impact*. Cheltenham, UK: Edward Elgar Publishing. https://doi.org/10.4337/9781784711856.000211

Boldrin, M., & Levine, D. K. (2008). *Against Intellectual Monopoly* (pp. 1–309). Cambridge: Cambridge University Press.

Boldrin, M., & Levine, D. K. (2013). The case against patents. *The Journal of Economic Perspectives, 27*(1), 3–22. http://doi.org/10.1257/jep.27

Brant, J., & Lohse, S. (2013). *Enhancing Intellectual Property Management and Appropriation by Innovative SMEs* (pp. 1–24). Paris: International Chamber of Commerce.

Caillaud, B., & Duchêne, A. (2011). Patent office in innovation policy: Nobody's perfect. *International Journal of Industrial Organization, 29*(2), 242–252. http://doi.org/10.1016/j.ijindorg.2010.06.002

Chen, J., Brem, A., Viardot, E., & Wong, P. K. (2019). *The Routledge Companion to Innovation Management*. Abington and New York: Routledge.

Cooter, R., & Ulen, T. (2016). *Law and Economics* (6 ed., pp. 1–570). Pearson Education Limited.

Ding, Y. (2013). Patent mediation: A robust choice for resolving patent disputes. *Disputes Resolution Journal, 68*(4), 87.

Eisenberg, R. S. (1996). Public research and private development: Patents and technology transfer in government-sponsored research. *Virginia Law Review, 82*(8), 1663–1727.

Elkin-Koren, N., & Salzberger, E. M. (2013). *The Law and Economics of Intellectual Property in the Digital Age* (pp. 1–305). New York: Routledge.

Fisher, W. W., III, & Oberholzer-Gee, F. (2013). Strategic management of intellectual property. *California Management Review, 55*(4), 157–183.

Foray, D. (2013). Patent-free innovation- a review of economic works including the analysis of a recent work in the field of experimental economics. *Revue Economique, 64*(1), 9–27.

Frakes, M. D., & Wasserman, M. F. (2019). Irrational ignorance at the patent office. *Vanderbilt Law Review, 72*, 975.

Gargate, G., Siddiquee, Q., & Wingkar, C. (2019). Intellectual property audit of an organization. *The Journal of World Intellectual Property, 22*(1–2), 16–35.

Grzegorczyk, T. (2020). Managing intellectual property: Strategies for patent holders. *The Journal of High Technology Management Research*, 100374.

Hausner, J. (2019). *Społeczna czasoprzestrzeń gospodarowania* (pp. 1–442). Warszawa: Wydawnictwo Nieoczywiste.

Hausner, J., & Zmyślony, M. (2015). *Firma idea - nowe podejście do wartości w biznesie* (pp. 1–37). Kraków: Fundacja GAP.

Kremer, M. (1998). Patent buyouts: A mechanism for encouraging innovation. *The Quarterly Journal of Economics, 113*(4), 1137–1167.

Krueger, A. B. (2019). *Rockonomics: A Backstage Tour of What the Music Industry Can Teach Us About Economics and Life.* Broadway Business.

Lallement, R. (2017). *Intellectual Property and Innovation Protection.* Hoboken, NJ: John Wiley & Sons. http://doi.org/10.1002/9781119473800

Lerner, J. (2005). 150 years of patent office practice. *American Law and Economics Review, 7*(1), 112–143. http://doi.org/10.1093/aler/ahi001

Oleksak, M. M., & Adams, M. (2010). *Intangible Capital* (pp. 1–192). Santa Barbara, CA: Praeger.

Porter, M. E., Michael, P., Kramer, M. R., & Kramer, M. R. (2011). Creating shared value. *Harvard Business Review*, 1–17.

Sampat, B. N. (2018). *A Survey of Empirical Evidence on Patents and Innovation.* Cambridge: National Bureau of Economic Research.

Stiglitz, J. E. (2008). Economic foundations of intellectual property rights. *Duke Law Journal, 57*(6), 1693–1724.

Treacy, P., & Lawrance, S. (2008). FRANDly fire: Are industry standards doing more harm than good? *Journal of Intellectual Property Law & Practice, 3*(1), 22–29.

World Intellectual Property Organization (WIPO). (2014). *Patent Pools and Antitrust - a Comparative Analysis* (pp. 1–18). WIPO.

Conclusion

It is highly erroneous to assume that effective legal protection of intellectual property is a condition necessary for development. Furthermore, many authors prove the correlation between those two variables to be rather weak (Boldrin & Levine, 2008, p. 134). A vivid example is the growth of the so-called dot-coms – businesses founded on Internet services at the turn of the century. At the early phase, patentability of software-based inventions was miniscule. Notwithstanding that, the market growth rate was very high and allowed authors of best constructs to earn huge profits. Moreover, development of virtual service platforms even allowed many companies to achieve almost monopolistic positions (mainly based on natural monopoly mechanisms). As a result, we now face a number of states similar in nature to a monopsony (Padilla, Ginsburg, & Wong-Ervin, 2019).

The story of dot-coms is most often referred to in the context of the investment bubble crash from the 2000s. One must, however, remember that was not the result of insufficient protection of intellectual property but huge deficits in the methods of assessment and valuation of those assets, which has been elaborated upon in the context of the causes of the Tragedy of Intangible Abundance. The problem was caused by the conviction that every Internet business must be a success story and the difference between the book value and market value almost always reflects exclusively the value of off-balance intangible assets. That bubble, however, did not burst because of imitation activities or software unpatentability. From the social perspective it is neither plausible to state that supply of dot-com services was unsatisfactory. In the context of the Tragedy of Intangible Abundance one may additionally observe the much better matching of demand and supply.

That story is thus a clear exit guide or the instruction to at least partially overcome the dysfunctions described in this book. In less regulated domains the emerging abundance is less constrained and, on the basis of competitive mechanisms, it adjusts to the market needs to a greater extent. Rejection of restrictive legal monopolies facilitates more fluid adaptation to changes and consumers' needs. Such an approach obviously generates substantially lower social costs too. The advantage of innovators over imitators is then built based on combination of the first copy holder privilege and natural monopoly creation mechanisms. At a later stage it may only be supported legally, e.g. through registered trademarks.

One must bear in mind that dissemination of some knowledge and its exploitation by third parties do not have to cause its creator to be deprived of the opportunity to earn from it. Furthermore, under specific conditions, the creator's privileged position may also remain unshakeable. That results from the fact that it is impossible to perfectly transfer the entire value creation process from one company to another. The number of variables is so vast that even unrestrained copying of all identified components will not guarantee success. Within this context, it bears noting that recipe books published by top cooks will indeed not make them jobless (Foray, 2013, p. 17). Furthermore, it does not only make them jobless but thanks to higher popularity it will give them the opportunity to earn more.

Therefore, the modern economy needs the combination of intellectual property and openness. Too many companies undertake a helpless fight for possibly most extensive protection of the exclusiveness of their intellectual property rights. That approach is bound to fail since it means fighting against easy copying that is the immanent feature of intellectual property. It is therefore better to treat that conditionality not as a threat but as an opportunity and take advantage of that as fuel for one's business models in order to build one's competitive advantage based on openness and widespread dissemination. As not only the future but also the present belong to 'the Economics of Intellectual Property and Openness'.

References

Boldrin, M., & Levine, D. K. (2008). *Against Intellectual Monopoly* (pp. 1–309). Cambridge: Cambridge University Press.

Foray, D. (2013). Patent-free innovation- a review of economic works including the analysis of a recent work in the field of experimental economics. *Revue Economique, 64*(1), 9–27.

Padilla, J., Ginsburg, D. H., & Wong-Ervin, K. (2019). Antitrust analysis involving intellectual property and standards: Implications from economics. *Harvard Journal of Law & Technology, 33*(1), 1–64.

Index

Note: **Bold** page numbers refer to tables and *italic* page numbers refer to figures.

Printed in the United States
by Baker & Taylor Publisher Services